Soft Leadership
for Hard Times

George A. Goens

Laura —
May the intangible forces of the
universe lead you to happiness
and quench your yearning. Spirit
lives, love thrives, and miracles
happen!

George A. Goens

ROWMAN & LITTLEFIELD EDUCATION
Lanham, Maryland • Toronto • Oxford
2005

Published in the United States of America
by Rowman & Littlefield Education
A Division of Rowman & Littlefield Publishers, Inc.
A wholly owned subsidary of The Rowman & Littlefield Publishing Group, Inc.
4501 Forbes Boulevard, Suite 200, Lanham, Maryland 20706
www.rowmaneducation.com

PO Box 317
Oxford
OX2 9RU, UK

British Library Cataloguing in Publication Information Available

Library of Congress Cataloging-in-Publication Data
Goens, George A.
  Soft leadership for hard times / George A. Goens.
     p. cm.
  Includes bibliographical references and index.
  ISBN 1-57886-252-3 (pbk. : alk. paper)
  1. Educational leadership. 2. Leadership. I. Title.
LB2805.G5385 2005
371.2—dc22

                                                    2004030971

⊖™ The paper used in this publication meets the minimum requirements of
American National Standard for Information Sciences—Permanence of
Paper for Printed Library Materials, ANSI/NISO Z39.48-1992.
Manufactured in the United States of America.

In loving memory of my daughter,
Betsy J. Bower,
who left this world all too soon.

In thanksgiving for my grandchildren,
Claire and Luke,
who are true reminders of the real meaning of life.

In love for and celebration of my son,
Curtis A. Goens,
who is a person of courage and integrity.

Contents

Contents

Acknowledgments

We enter and leave this world alone, but we live life with others. I am grateful for the relationships I have had with my professional colleagues in Wisconsin and Connecticut. I have learned so very much from my association with them in the good and the difficult times. They have provided insight and wisdom—and I respect their dedication, leadership, and work.

I have been blessed with wonderful friends. They have stayed with me when I made blunderous errors: they have always stood by my side holding my spirit in their hands. They laugh with me in joyous times, cry with me when deep tragedy strikes, and forgive me when I err. I don't even know how to thank them. I wish I could name them all here . . . but they know who they are. Bless you all.

I owe a special thanks to my business partner, Lou Esparo, who helped me start a new and exciting phase of my life. He is more than a partner—he is a great, caring friend. We met through the serendipitous nature of life and I have been enriched.

Over ten years ago, Marcia Spector asked me to work with her to design and create small, innovative schools for the children in Milwaukee. What started out as an opportunity turned into a friendship of trust and respect tied together with work of deep meaning.

Ideas blossom in conversation. My special conversations with my friends Bud and Emmy Theisen and Rachel Boechler provided insight into life and leadership. William F. Paton gave me my first opportunity to explore leadership and has been a great model and mentor. Thank you.

Mary Stevenson read portions of the manuscript and offered insightful and challenging comments. She provided needed and welcomed encouragement in frustrating times. She has a wonderful aura of goodness about her.

I also want to thank Ashley Dove, a high school student, who typed some of the early chapters, deciphering my illegible handwriting.

Most of this book was written on Peter and Eileen Litwin's farm in Litchfield, Connecticut. It is truly a magical place, with spiritual and creative energy flowing through each blade of grass and brimming from each stone. Thank you for allowing me to share it and to live in the "small farmhouse."

I owe so much to my son, Curtis. He will never know how much he has helped me. Sons do not always see their impact on their parents. He has a good heart and has an old soul that guides him with wisdom.

Finally, Betsy, my daughter, died while I was writing this book. She and I were much alike in many ways. I found that in her spiritual studies, she was contemplating the same values and principles that I was investigating while working on this project. She found her calling as a mother and pursued it with joy and deep passion. I miss her deeply.

I give thanks every day for Claire and Luke, my grandchildren, who remind me of times past and the gift and promise of each new day.

1

Introduction: Leadership and Paradox

A desk is a dangerous place from which to view the world.

—John Le Carré

The life of a leader is a precarious one, as it should be. Leaders should not walk the shores of certainty and comfort. It is not their way. True leaders face life and make themselves known to the world. They do not sit on the warm, grassy slopes of anonymity and simply observe. They get involved with their hearts, souls, and spirit to make dreams and principles a reality.

Leadership is critical to successful ventures. Each year hundreds of books on leadership are published. They offer practical tips that can be employed in a "minute" to alter circumstances. They proffer strategies. They talk of getting to the bottom line. They advocate styles of leadership from Jesus to Patton as templates. Others suggest managing for results, leading with jazz, leading in one minute, or reengineering, which presupposes you engineered once. This bevy of books provides suggestions, processes, and approaches to help leaders get results. The books elevate the leader as hero. The problem is that the all-knowing, controlling, cool, and decisive savior–leader may be a figment of our imaginations nourished by myths and contemporary culture.

Most of these books view leadership from a mechanical or technical perspective as a means of curing or fixing organizational maladies. In that regard, they trade on a perception that may not be valid in an uncertain world that is not easily controlled by human beings. The world and the people in it do not always succumb to the strategies of a leader or the tweaking of a strategic plan. Scientific management falls short in a nonrational environment.

Our society has had a love affair with science. Back in the 1960s we met the Soviet Sputnik challenge through masterful engineering. We believed that science applied through engineering concepts and data could solve our problems. Consequently, we learned how to create flow charts, make time lines, map critical paths, and execute other linear and sequential approaches to problem solving. We thought we could engineer ourselves out of problems and program excellence into organizations. In those times, things seemed neat, simple, and logical. That trend is alive and well in strategic planning and total quality management approaches, and the metrical analysis of just about everything from political opinions to student achievement.

Our new religion, it seems, is science and engineering, as we look to laboratories to help make our lives happier, to hold on to our youth, or to "connect" to the world through a computer screen. We have Botox for smoothing our wrinkles and fighting the signs of aging, pills to keep us thin and happy, and technology to keep us occupied and connected. Today we even talk of bioengineering, cloning, and creating "designer" babies. Certainly, medical science and technology can be helpful, but the answers to life do not come out of a bottle, laboratory, or our C-drives.

It is not unreasonable, then, to think we can "re-engineer" ourselves into productive organizations, excellent schools, or a better body. The perception exists that all leaders need to do is analyze and diagnose the problem, break it into manageable parts, pick metrically measurable goals, implement specific strategies, and voilà!—we produce successful and productive enterprises. In this approach, rational, scientific, and strategic approaches are all a leader requires in order to succeed.

This book takes a different perspective. The world is a place of wonder that is unpredictable and serendipitous, filled with paradox and ambiguity. It can be messy and volatile, enrapturing people with indescribable beauty, and yet also be brutal and fierce. Patterns exist but not always certainty. It is a place where human control is limited and where dreams, unseen forces, and fields sway nations and defy logic. It is the place where leaders—in every sense and breadth of the word—reside and are needed.

As a result, in the world of schools, the times feel hard. We blanch at the sting of rejection and we feel adrift on the turbulent tides of politics and society, complete with contradictory expectations and demands. Politicians, taxpayers, and parents call out for the tough and hard leadership of our mythology. The illusions of "leadership past" hang like yokes around the necks of people who accept the challenge of teaching, running a school, or leading a district. They face heroic expectations that cannot be met overnight. The demands for quick fixes, quick results, and quick action haunt those who try to conscientiously address the perplexing problems facing schools.

In this context leaders fear appearing soft and not up to the task. They desire to fix things. They vow to do things. They want to cure things. They push, trying to make things happen. They line up ducks, they grease the gears, they put the machinery in motion, they plan strategically and define benchmarks, they collect and mine data, and they create regulations and procedures to pull productivity and commitment out of the people who work for them. They are hard drivers who try to find the secret that will unlock the mysteries of the organizations they lead.

In the process, leaders have forgotten about the words that were connected in the past with the place called school: joy, imagination, creativity, compassion, beauty, liberty, truth, goodness, and wisdom. The naysayers will caution, "How do you measure virtues? What metric are you going to use?" If you cannot measure results, it does not matter. Virtues are too soft to count in the real world.

But what is the real world? It is not a machine. A board of directors did not construct it. It does not run like a watch or a computer. It is not predictable and does not succumb to the whims of men and women who wish to direct and manage it. It is deaf to human commands and blind to directives even though we try to "master" it.

Physicists discovered that the nature of things in the universe rests on relationships and patterns. A natural order exists in the real world—seasons come and go, weather stirs through in cycles, life moves through stages, and the earth renews itself without our prodding. The real world is organic, self-organizing; and although chaos reigns at times, there is an orderly rhythm to life and an interconnectivity that works in harmony in the universe.

Leaders can learn from the natural world, but we seem stuck in finding the mainspring—the key—that controls everything. The soft issues in leadership can produce great things if we do not act in mechanistic and artificial ways. Soft leadership may be more in harmony with the real world of relationships than the mechanistic Newtonian approaches that see the universe as a great machine that will perform with logical precision if we can find the right variables.

You don't succeed for very long by kicking people around. You've got to know how to talk to them, plain and simple.

—Lee Iacocca, former CEO, Ford Motor Company

We have a real problem with language. The problem is the use of the words *soft* and *hard*, which carry charged connotations, particularly as they relate to organizations and leadership. Words are important because they establish mindsets, mental pictures, or perceptions that reflect how we interpret the world. These mindsets have positive or negative charges.

When it comes to leadership, *hard* frequently connotes tough, hard-nosed, no-nonsense, strong, and single-minded. The hard-driving CEO is a part of our organizational folklore, frequently spawned by the leader-as-hero books and a media addicted to the cult of personality and celebrity. *Tough*, however, also has other connotations: difficult, strict, and hard, along with the associated synonyms of rigid, stern, inflexible, and taxing.

Soft, on the other hand, has a very negative nuance in organizational parlance. *Leadership* and *softness* are not used in the same sentence. *Softness* has a bad name because it is associated with weakness, flabbiness, indecisiveness, mushiness, and wimpishness. Just think of the term *soft-headed* and a picture erupts of a squashy, uncertain, and malleable person who cannot take a stand or think for him- or herself. Softness is associated with cowardice and shrinking in the face of challenge.

To some, *hard* involves tangibles and metrics—numbers. Hard data can be measured, seen, and counted, and they are perceived as objective. For many, hard data relates to the bottom line—if you cannot measure or see it, it does not exist, or, to some, it is not very important. Leaders often say, "What are the numbers?" Schools are being assessed on this altar of measurability. The logic goes: Schools are successful if they produce the right numbers—high test scores, positive attendance rates, high graduation rates, low dropout rates, and so forth.

On the other hand, people die for such soft and difficult-to-quantify concepts as justice, liberty, equality, and truth. The intangibles of morale, satisfaction, and motivation stalk and obsess leaders working in failing organizations. Without them, productivity sags and metrics suffer. Helping people find their place, their voice, and their contributions are at the essence of leadership. Those are the things that cause each of us to feel connected to each other in a common enterprise and move us away from the sense that we are just cogs in a wheel. People desire to follow a calling, not just do a job. We all want to feel connected to one another and engaged in important work. We reject that we are simply interchangeable parts plodding aimlessly in isolation.

The old connotations of *hard* and *soft* must be addressed for a conversation about leadership to take place. Examining definitions and language uncovers the deeper meaning of words and phrases. For example, soft leadership is *not*:

- Indecisiveness
- Meekness
- Fearfulness
- Avoidance
- Sappiness
- Emotionalism
- Weakness

In life, it seems, paradox is our companion. The same is true with *soft* and *tough* when it comes to leadership. The irony is the so-called hard leadership approaches of the past may be the easiest to implement; and the soft approaches to leadership may be the hardest to employ because they strike at the very heart of life with its splendor and frustration.

Being uncompromising, hard, and directing is the easiest form of management. While not always pleasant, it is the safest course for people in administrative positions because they strictly enforce regulations and do not have to betray themselves as human beings. They simply play the part and hide behind a role, while focusing on consistent processes and superordinate controls and rules. Making people tow the mark is easy, particularly if you have the power to take retribution and impose punishment. Driving and pushing people may be frustrating, but it is not difficult, and for short bursts of time, people may be moved in a particular direction by this approach. Being hard-nosed can be the easiest, weakest, and most destructive approach a leader can take because it does not add long-term value or nurture creativity.

The Chinese philosopher Lao Tzu wrote about hardness and softness:

> Living people
> are soft and tender.
> Corpses are hard and stiff.
> The ten thousand things,
> the living grass, the trees,
> are soft and pliant.
> Dead, they are dry and brittle.
>
> So hardness and stiffness
> go with death;
> tenderness, softness,
> go with life.
>
> And the hard sword fails,
> the stiff tree's felled.
> The hard and great go under.
> The soft and weak stay up.[1]

In a day when hardness and toughness are associated with strength, Lao Tzu's insight reminds us that suppleness and flexibility will survive rigidity. Soft leadership is not weakness—quite the reverse. It requires the biggest risk leaders can take—revealing themselves in an authentic way, complete with the vulnerabilities of their unique humanness. Some athletes are said to have soft hands. Under pressure, they can catch blistering, hard throws or they can make shots that require finesse, sensitivity, and care. Metaphorically, leaders need soft hands, too, to deal with the complex challenges they face.

This softness is about being subtle, sensitive, flexible, open, approachable, and perceptive. It is not foisting emotions on people, being smarmy, or breeching the normal barriers of propriety we all maintain. Soft leadership boils down to:

- Knowing yourself and being self-reflective
- Taking the risk to be your true self in leading others—living your values, principles, and beliefs
- Understanding that leadership does not reside in one position or person
- Helping others fulfill themselves and reach their potential
- Breaking barriers and artificial walls that separate people
- Being vulnerable—all aspects of truthfulness, as a leader, being comfortable in your own shoes, and not role-playing
- Recognizing the ability of ordinary people to do extraordinary things
- Seeing connections and interrelationships between people and the natural order of things
- Recognizing that structures are more than roles—they are also values, ethics, norms, and principles
- Seeing people as individuals, with ideas, emotions, gifts, and energy
- Understanding that everything that can be counted may not count in the greater order of things
- Knowing that the human spirit can be noble, creative, imaginative, and selfless
- Recognizing the power of intangibles in life

Soft leadership from this perspective can produce bottom-line results: desirable outcomes, increased productivity, and motivated people. We all want to belong to an enterprise in which we can use our talent to serve and to act as stewards of the common good.

Poetry is a metaphor for leading in today's difficult world—filled with ambiguity and uncertainty and connected through a subtle, transparent, and complex web of relationships and dimensions. Leadership addresses the human longing to serve, to pursue a calling, to be able to do one's work, and to have our individual and collective voices heard in the world. Life's journey is about finding ourselves, our hearts, and our spirits, as well as developing our minds. Efficacy is what is needed in schools and organizations. Empowerment comes from a sense of efficacy—of understanding our ability to contribute and knowing how we can belong to our work and world. It is about knowing how we fit in relationship to our destiny.

Leadership requires all of our capabilities; particularly those that can bring people together around a common purpose so positive and wonderful things can happen. We see it vividly in crisis when people self-organize, get the job done, care for each other and commit to the common good. Deep relationships and ties develop in these circumstances, and people feel that they are in it together.

Leaders and poets are tightly connected in spirit. Leaders and engineers are distant, distant cousins. The world calls for leadership that helps us all be the people we are called to be. It is not about controlling, appealing to the lowest common denominator, or assuming we are all motivated by selfish interests. Leaders nurture relationships and commitment and help create integral organizations that are connected through purpose and stewardship.

This book speaks to leadership and the poetry leaders bring to people in perplexing times and highlights some ways in which that organizational poetry can be written. Leaders engage others in a conversation about high ideals. They try to identify ways in which that conversation can be held and how our lives at work can be rewarding and fulfilling. School leaders call on us to use our creative energy and human spirit to do noble and good things.

NOTE

1. Lao Tzu. "Hardness." In *Lao Tzu: Tao Te Ching*, translated by Ursula K. Le Guin. Boston: Shambhala Publications, 1997, p. 96.

2

Leadership and Poetry

Aren't there moments that are better than knowing something, and sweeter?

—Mary Oliver

Poets and leaders grapple with the same mysteries of life. In fact, all of us do. We just don't recognize or perceive them as part of the great stage on which life plays out.

We usually think of the context of our life in an external way: examining what is outside ourselves. The times are said to make leaders, as if we were bystanders to a play unfolding around us. We think the important setting is "out there" in the greater world. Certainly in the external world—our society and institutions—relationships are a part of the context of our existence. Leadership, however, does not exist solely in the social, political, and economic world. There is more, something sweeter, that moves beyond simply knowing systems, strategies, and concepts—something greater and much more personal that gets at the internal essence of who we are.

Leadership has both an inner dimension and an external one. These outer and inner domains affect our lives personally and professionally. Like poets who observe and comment on the natural world, leaders toil in the fields of day-to-day life, with its crises, interactions, and purpose. They try to understand the dynamics of the push and pull of events and happenings. Poets, however, do more.

Poets also explore the unknown, the mystical, the spiritual, and the mysterious dimensions inside us. They raise questions: Who are we? Why are we here? What are we called to do? What is inside of us? Where do heart, spirit, and soul come into play in life? What is the purpose of our journey? What is the meaning and significance of all of this?

Poets observe the interconnected nature of us in both the inner and outer worlds. They ponder our relationships with others and the universe. They marvel at the simplicity and beauty of our world, and the intense desire, emotion, and feeling we have in this life.

Poets muse on life—its purpose, its significance, its wonder, its beauty, its genius, its travails, its pain, its conflict. Poets and other artists help us define ourselves with respect to others and the universe, and they help us see and marvel at the gift of life in bright or dark times. They help define life's noble ventures, and remind us of the simple beauty of nature and importance of human tenderness. They speak of soul and spirit.

Great leaders do the same. They use symbolic and other gestures to rally people around honorable and good causes. They inspire people to reach for a higher calling and direct people's attention to the critical issues of living, working, and belonging.

Leadership has a moral dimension, and the ends and means must have the same harmonic structure. Leaders must select strategies that are in harmony with principles to ensure integrity and credibility.

Leaders and poets both work the soil of intangibles—those things in life that are hard to measure but make us uniquely human and alive. Leadership is not an emotionless endeavor, because leaders connect with the heartstrings of people to nourish insight, wonder, creativity, and motivation. Poets and leaders live in intimate relationship with the minds, hearts, and souls of people. Sometimes that life is harsh or tender, noble or crass, quiet or bombastic. Leaders and poets touch us in ways that help us see our existence and ourselves more clearly and sometimes with a unique perspective.

Poetry frequently provides insight on the simple things of life. The call to simplicity is legendary in literature, poetry, and philosophy. Leaders' lives seem consumed by the surrounding context and its complex trials. Yet, leaders, while yearning for simplicity, must make intricate issues known and understandable in simple terms to others. Leaders unite people in common purpose to respond to this environment.

Bathed in complex challenges, leaders do not always need to know what to do or how things will work. However, they must face issues truthfully regardless of personal price or cost—success or failure—if they are to help people see how those people can contribute. At times leaders may do simple things or nothing at all—because that is all they can do in a messy world. The simplicity of living an authentic and truthful life with integrity and peaceful resolve is the only virtue leaders have when things are confusing.

The old Shaker hymn "Simple Gifts" reminds us that in simplicity there is freedom and a sense of peace and efficacy.

> 'Tis the gift to be simple, 'tis the gift to be free;
> 'Tis the gift to come down where we ought to be;
> And when we find ourselves in the place just right,
> 'Twill be in the valley of love and delight.
>
> When true simplicity is gained,
> To bow and to bend we shan't be ashamed
> To turn, turn will be our delight,
> 'Til by turning, turning we come 'round right.[1]

Finding "where we ought to be" in our life and work is a true gift. In today's atmosphere, we can spin our lives in layers of involvement and tiers of actions, reactions, proactions, and distress. Finding our place and calling in clear, simple terms in a chaotic environment frees us to be ourselves to meet our destiny—the place where things fit and feel just right. Simplicity, getting to the core and cutting through the confounding swamps of politics and procedures, is the true art and hallmark of both leadership and poetry in creating meaning.

There is no script to life, and heroes and villains are not always in clear focus. Good leaders invoke wonder and a whole range of other emotions when they share their truth. Like poets, the risk is in allowing people to see your thoughts and beliefs; with this risk comes great human vulnerability because the hurt of rejection is more personal.

Man is an over-complicated organism. If he is doomed to extinction, he will die out for want of simplicity.

—Ezra Pound

Being vulnerable is what many leaders fear, seeing it as a limitation and danger. Being vulnerable, however, is an important part of leadership if you are to trust people and put a human face on responsibilities and obligations. The irony is that leaders desire to touch people's lives but want to do so from the antiseptic, closed cocoon of an organizational hierarchy, away from the vulnerability of genuine openness, interaction, and candor.

Vulnerability simply means taking responsibility. Leaders who are courageous put themselves on the line and take responsibility. In many organizations, deflecting responsibility or pointing the finger of blame at others is the norm. When they make a decision, vulnerable leaders open themselves to criticism and avoid defensiveness. When a leader is open, sensitive, and thoughtful, people are inclined to believe the strength and force of the leader's position. Dancing around issues, dodging responsibility for actions, and not facing people directly when things are tough generates cynicism and doubt. Walking straight into adversity takes strength because the wall of isolation between leaders and those they lead collapses. Unexpected feelings and "undiscussables"—those elephants in the room people ignore because of discomfort or fear—are uncovered. This type of vulnerability takes boldness and courage.

Finally, life is not an exercise in engineering in that it follows a logical or sequential path. Life is filled with whimsy and mystery, serendipity and synchronicity. The unanticipated frequently hands us the biggest challenges, the largest gifts, and the greatest satisfaction. Being open to these situations is how leaders shine. The celebration of life, for poets and leaders, is about confronting our yearning for belonging and finding our calling as unique individuals. This takes place in both the internal and external worlds.

THE CONTEXTS OF LEADERSHIP

Two Worlds

For us there are Two Worlds of Being.
The First World is the outer world we live in,
A shell that encases the body, an attitude
That stifles the mind and pretends
That money is the measure of worth.

The First World is harsh, though comfortable,
Alluring, though vain. It is the popular world
Where everyone longs to be, yet once they arrive,
They dream of a new direction. In this world,
Everything costs something and what is free costs more.

The First World is one of wheels and destinations,
Membership dues and limitations. It is a sanctuary
For those who desire conformity in all things.
Here duplicate people wearing duplicate clothes
Speak a language without meaning, and think thoughts
Without substance to their form.

The First World is where everyone lives, yet
No one actually survives. It is an acceptable address
Where you forfeit all that you are for what
You will never become and what you are not
Is what you want those around you to remember.

The First World has power, but no strength.
It is one of mirrors, but no reflection.
In this world, there is success, but no mystery.
Goals, but no journey. In this world,
Boundaries keep ideas from colliding.

The Second World is the world of inner harmony,
Where you can go anytime your spirit aches for company.
Here you can listen to the songs of rocks and leaves and
Embrace the wisdom of rivers and essential things contained in
Raindrops or a flower's belly or the earth's warm breath of spring.
In this world, beauty is companion to mystery.

The Second World is one of joy and curiosity,
A connecting thread to birds and oceans, plants and animals.
The Second World is one of children's laughter, women's songs,
Men's stories, the essence that remains long after the experience
Has passed on. In this world, all circles return.

The Second World is where you can travel
On the wings of dreams or the tails of newborn stars.
This world is revealed through a rainbow's colored eyes,
Or in a spider's silver road between two leaves,
Or even in silence, the kind that follows ecstasy.

The Second World is able to survive without the First,
But the First World cannot last long without the Second.
The Second World offers meaning to existence
While the First World offers existence only.

Between these two Worlds
Lies reason, the seam that connects one World to another.
The Second World is yours for no money.
The First World is yours for no effort.
Which one will you choose?

—Nancy Wood[2]

   Leaders live each day in these two worlds. They face all the pressures, emptiness, and allures of the First World and they yearn for the meaning of the Second. Our culture created the First World, and some would say it is constructed on a shaky perception of human nature grounded in greed, competitiveness, and materialism. For cynics, this is the so-called real world. This dark and dangerous view of human nature permeates relationships, decisions, and protocols in the First World.

We frequently think that this First World is the "practical" one—the valid one. On the other hand, the Second World appears fanciful, idealistic, and unrealistic. This seems odd because, as life ebbs from our pores, we long for a final grasp at the Second World—children's laughter, our embrace of loved ones, or seeing a rainbow for the last time. I doubt we will hunger for another board meeting or receiving another perk or wall plaque. So, really, what is reality?

Many leaders feel more comfortable in the First than the Second World. Rules appear to be clearer, issues seemingly can be resolved, and personal liability is limited because we live behind the mask of our roles as we posture on the social, political, or economic stage. The Second World is less tangible, but understanding it is absolutely essential for compassionate and noble leaders and a life worth living.

THE FIRST WORLD

We constructed the First World's reality, and it is reflected in the way we do business, the manner in which we interact, and the pace and focus of our lives. Not all cultures across the globe exist in our "reality" of the First World. People in some other cultures choose to live and relate to one another and their institutions based on a different view of the world. This First World reality feeds off our ego needs and our attachments to worldly and materialistic things.

We succumb to worldly things because of our need for belonging. Aloneness in our society is frightening to some. We think that because we are by ourselves we are alone and disconnected. If we accumulate wealth, have a healthy batch of certificates and awards pasted on our walls, and drive the latest version of the "I made it" car, then we belong to a group of "successful" people, and have the tangible proof to show it. Status, wealth, and image matter more to some than does the substance of a principled life with deep and authentic connections to people and a concern for issues greater than our own self-interest.

The drive to achieve status and material goods is rooted in our ego and in trying to reach the expectations of others. Parents, spouses, or others may have expectations of us that are not part of our destiny. We get lost in doing and living what others expect of us—not always realizing we have but one life to lead—our own. Living to please others may not please anyone at all, especially ourselves. Living a life driven by ego becomes hollow.

The mythological view is of a leader who is an independent individual, who is his or her "own person." Yet, paradoxically, to win favor and survive in the First World, conforming and molding ourselves to "propriety" and the expectations of others are valued. Speaking, dressing, thinking, eating, and behaving imprison people of the First World with the chains of what is "appropriate" and accepted. They don't become their own people. In this context, leaders adopt vanilla personalities and pursue goals that alienate the fewest possible people. Politicians are known for posturing and trying to govern by public opinion polls. In the process of not trying to alienate anyone, they compromise their values and undermine their leadership standing.

In the First World, we create rules or axioms designed to help us "get ahead." In many cases, these rules are dysfunctional and contrary to the essence of leadership. Some of them include:

- *"We go along . . . to get along"* and, as a consequence, we implement the rule of self-censorship. We don't say what's on our mind in order to be accepted and not upset the organizational "apple cart." We go along to belong to the group or club of colleagues or influentials. We do not want to be the wolf howling in the wilderness. In the process, we may not be true to ourselves, and consequently, we collide with our conscience and suffer not speaking and living our truth.
- *"We play the game,"* which is an outgrowth of getting along, requiring manipulation, deflecting responsibility, and avoiding direct conflict. If life is a game, then winning and looking good is important. "Getting the edge," even by cutting corners, and cleverness are advantageous. Frequently, military or sports metaphors are used about work—mobilizing forces, strategizing, dying on hills, falling on swords, blitzing, and multifrontal strategies are all examples of gamesmanship mentality.

  In playing games, however, the things that become all-important are competition, not cooperation; analysis, not synthesis; individualism, not collaboration; and tangibles, not intangibles. Balance and relationships become lost in reaching "targets" and beating the competition. Ego reigns. If we don't play, we are fearful that we will "bomb" in leading and become failures cast out into the cold.
- In playing the game, *"we don't want to be loved, we want to be respected."* We play for keeps, keep score, and believe that what goes around comes around. Getting to the right bottom line is all-important, no matter what road we take to get there or the means we use. The emotional tenor is generally negative. The major sentiments are retribution, not forgiveness; fear, not affection; and revenge, not reconciliation. On this emotional edge, a life is lived in desperation, loneliness, and detachment. If life is a game to be won, maybe that is why some leaders feel it is lonely at the top or fear being challenged and criticized. Winning is personal, and failure is fatal.
- Finally, the First World is one filled with influence, not the creative genius of people. It is *"who you know, not what you know."* The "winners"

are in the circle of influence; the losers are on the outside. The landscape is filled with mutual back-scratching and bootlicking, influence following cash, and power following position. Power is seen as finite and needs to be hoarded and controlled, while leaders play things close to the vest and do not betray their motives or connections. Relationships become manipulative "contacts" and are based on influence. If the perceived power is lost, the relationship dissolves: Why waste time with people who cannot promote personal success and moving up the ladder?

The First World confronts conflict with power, cleverness, spin, and force. Disequilibrium does not fit the tightly controlled plans and strategies designed to increase conformity to achieve a desired statistical bottom line, or to build egos.

The backdrop for leadership in the First World is economic, political, and social systems. This world values certainty and clarity. To be successful, there has to be the appearance of control, which is one of life's great illusions. In either world, getting control and keeping it is impossible. Control is an ephemeral concept because we have power over so little. Life's ebbs and flows keep disturbing our plans, making our life less predictable and filled with surprises. As David Whyte states in the poem "What to Remember When Waking,"

> . . . What you can plan
> is too small
> for you to live.
>
> What you can live
> wholeheartedly
> will make plans
> enough
> for the vitality
> hidden in your sleep.[3]

Following a calling or ideals may open doors never thought of in our plans. The serendipitous world and our hearts may lead us to a greater destiny, if we are open and can listen to it. Whyte highlights that our linear, strategically designed plans fall short of the greatness that can await us. Our plans, each with measurable objectives, may actually restrict us from larger issues and tie us to the administratively mundane, creating the dysfunction of major issues becoming minor and minor issues becoming major. We can lose sight of our vision.

In our daily plans we think the world is a rational place where every action has an equal reaction. In the First or Second World, we know that sometimes there's no reaction at all, or that the butterflies of life flap their wings and create forceful gusts and windstorms that change everything. The reactions of people cannot be predicted because we don't know the inner colors and textures of their Second World or understand the free will that barks from their soul.

> We must be willing to get rid of the life we've planned, so as to have the life that is waiting for us.
>
> —Joseph Campbell

The predictability of life is scant. Peoples' biographies are replete with synchronicity and accidents of fate. Insignificant events become major, and random luck, good or bad, can alter the roads we travel. While it may be helpful to chart a course for your career or life, enjoy the trip, because surprises abound, and the clockwork world you envision has a rhythm and nature all its own that is totally immune to your directives. Fifty years later you will look back and see the magic of life reflected in the lines on your face and alive in the rich memories and stories in your heart of pain and joy and the integral nature of humanity.

If life were predictable it would always be responsive to detailed planning and analysis. Every problem would succumb to the logic of the scientific method. All of the pieces of the puzzle would fall into place. The problem with life is "missing pieces" and inexplicable reactions to events. If logic and data ruled, we would have won the Vietnam War, and a World War I lunatic corporal would not have led one of the world's most cultured and sophisticated nations to ruin.

Finally, the First World honors degrees and pedigrees. The head—with its steel-eyed logic—is revered, and matters of the heart such as love, compassion, and forgiveness are seldom mentioned. They are seen as softheaded, not tough enough for the dog-eat-dog First World of competition and scrambling to the proverbial top. Showing your emotions is akin to revealing weakness. Keep things close to the vest. Stay cool and float on the cloud of objective logic, far above the fears and emotions of corporate or personal life.

The First World is a world of systems that are designed to manage it. Leaders work in systems in which their organizational lives are sliced into roles and role expectations. Organizational theorists talk of social systems theory and the head-on collision of the person with the organization. In particular, the expectations of others become a large factor in First World life. The trouble is that there is not one expectation, but multiple ones. With multiple expectations come conflict and the dicey reality of incongruence. Role conflict explodes, and deciding whose expectations you meet becomes frustrating and possibly corrupting if your ideals are sold out.

The poet Pablo Neruda, in his poem "Emerging," defines what happens better than any researcher.

> A man says yes without knowing
> how to decide even what the question is,
> and is caught up, and then carried along
> and never escapes again from his own cocoon;
> and that's how we are, forever falling
> into the deep well of other beings;
> and one thread wraps itself around our necks,
> another entwines a foot, and then it is impossible,
> impossible to move except in the well—
> nobody can rescue us from other people.[4]

The First World is geared to the desire to conform to the expectations and approval of others so we get salary, position, status, and ego-driven acclaim. In the process, we can lose ourselves—sell our souls to the system by being driven to perform to win others' approval and satisfaction. We barter our principles and unique creativity to win admiration and inclusion.

All of this can lead to exasperation and unhappiness. If we do not know ourselves, then when we reach sixty years old we won't recognize the ideals or dreams that sang from our hearts twenty-five years earlier. The person in the mirror will be a stranger, a hollow image of lost potential and unrealized ideals.

Conflict—positive conflict—between the First World and the Second World is monumental and inevitable. In our hearts we long for meaning, significance, and love. In following our life's calling, we also need forgiveness and compassion. Happiness and satisfaction with who we are in relation to our inner core and to others is essential. As we make ourselves known in the world, these are the challenges of the Second World.

THE SECOND WORLD—THE INNER WORLD

We also live in the inner and invisible Second World that inevitably collides with the First. Leaders bring to their work who they are as people, complete with heart, soul, and spirit, as well as their experience, hopes, fears, passions, and foibles.

The inner context defines who we are and who we want to be and affects our relationship to and in the outside world. We must answer questions about ourselves. What am I here for? What is meaningful? What is significant to me? What are my core principles? Am I a victim? A player? A dropout? A pawn? A manipulator? Am I authentic or inauthentic?

All of us who reflect are in the process of answering the question of who we are inside—examining the bright and dark sides of our souls. Who we are, what gives us meaning, and what our purpose is shape our relationships and the value we place on how we approach the First World.

In the First World, we often equate leadership with action: doing things and making things happen. We press and push and nudge and leverage things to have an impact, to be dynamic and vital. We confuse motion with movement and pushing with progress. Stillness and silence are infrequent visitors in the First World of power and influence, in which technology, information systems, and data reign.

Our spirit calls for something else. The rancorous pace and turmoil of material life take their toll. The cackling on cell phones and the deluge of e-mails wear us out. Instant access becomes disquieting and stressful. We yearn for quiet, stillness, and solitude—those things we can find in the Second World of rainbows, birds, the ebb and flow of the surf, or the tenderness of our children's hugs.

> In solitude we give passionate attention to our memories, to the details around us.
>
> —Virginia Woolf

In our action-oriented world, the question is: Are stillness and solitude action? Are they doing something? Can going inside to the quiet corner of our heart be considered action? Does action have to be overt and aggressive?

Action does not always require monumental moves or grandiose schemes. Sometimes the subtleness of action is not seen by the naked eye. Its movement may be unobservable, or it may be doing nothing at all. Action does not have to be flamboyant. Even in physical activities, subtle action frequently makes the difference between greatness and mediocrity. In music, silence—the rests—gives sound its dramatic impact and resonance.

Going inside yourself as a leader is an action, even though it's a solitary and invisible act. Finding silence, however, can make the difference in finding our truth by providing an opportunity to gain balance, to see nuances, to put things in their proper place. Silence, solitude, and reflection are critical for leaders, particularly in a fast-moving technological society. That's another great paradox: in a fast-moving world, slowing down and finding silence and solitude can be a great advantage in moving quickly toward success.

A critical link exists between the inner and outer worlds. Can a leader be effective in the First World if he or she is not at peace in the inner world? The mayhem of the external world creates pressure for visible action, but will that action be prudent and wise if the leader is in inner turmoil? The Second World of curiosity, joy, and harmony are essential to inner peace and helping leaders find balance. Leadership requires listening to our internal voice and to our intuitive senses, both of which are invaluable when we are in the throes of conflict. Feeling connected to our inner core and to something greater than ourselves gives us perspective on First World issues and allows us to develop an inner calmness in addressing them. The Second World is where we nourish our spirit and soul and find the courage to resist ego and false idols. Meaning and our significance are found here.

When we think of leadership, we seldom consider the inner or Second World. It is as if who the leader is as a human being is not important. Instead, we focus on what leaders "do," even though "doings" fall flat without the intangible spirit that comes from within. Otherwise, we would need only a simple blueprint or roadmap, and suddenly we would become leaders and our organizations would flourish. The Second World is the place where dreams are born, and where gossamer wings of determination and commitment help us fly—where our inner light guides us. The human spirit and vital sources of life roam the known and unknown terrain of our souls.

Our Second World is the crucial core of leadership because it reflects our humanity and life force based in moral values and principles. Integrity rests in our inner lives as leaders, requiring that we know our core values and define the ground on which we stand as individuals. We need to know what sod we call our own and what we will not compromise in confronting our destiny. Leaders can stand alone if that sod is grounded in integrity and principle.

Our character resides in the Second World within our heart and soul, but it manifests itself in the First World. Leadership is not solely an intellectual act. Einstein said, "We should take care not to make the intellect our god. It has, of course, powerful muscles, but no personality. It cannot lead, it can only serve."[5] Our character helps us navigate through the treacherous waters of conflict and the seductions of the First World. The inner context of leadership is where conscience and action collide and where knowledge and values and principles rub shoulders. Knowledge applied without moral principles can be disastrous; moral principles with no voice are hollow.

Finding one's truth and living within it are essential. Vaclav Havel, former president of the Czech Republic, writes, "Living within the truth . . . is an attempt to gain control over one's sense of responsibility."[6] We, as leaders, must find our truth—to ourselves, to our calling, to others— and to live *within* it if we are to be genuine people who are authentic and credible as leaders. Platitudes, empty gestures, or public relations cannot mask our insincerity or role-playing.

In our inner world, we also deal with losses and desires. It is the place our experiences come to rest their mantle of purpose and principle. True learning and growth come when we take experiences and emotions to heart— feel them, embrace them, and sense them. When we do, we face our fears and anxieties about who we are and how we fit in the world: then the pain of life becomes manageable. The Second World is the place where we cannot hide from the truth or from ourselves. Our quiet moments reveal who we are, with our merits and blemishes, and that mirror reflection is essential for wise and authentic leadership.

BOTH WORLDS

Leaders live in both worlds. Those who are at peace with themselves will not succumb to the whims and manipulations of the First World and others. They will act with integrity. To do so, however, leaders need to identify those principles in their lives that are not negotiable. The extent to which principles are compromised is the extent to which there are no principles. Knowing where to stand, as an individual, is important because not all conflicts are vital, and leaders define themselves by the issues they confront and the principles they pursue.

In the Second World, strength is more important than power. History shows us that brute power cannot overcome personal strength of purpose and integrity. Individuals face the world with all its harshness and survive by being strong of heart and resilient. Powerful people imprisoned many great leaders—Mandela, Havel, and King. Yet these leaders prevailed because of strength of purpose and integrity to principles.

To lead from your inner core is to serve others with honor. Leaders with strength act with honor in all their actions, and they respect and dignify life and the human spirit. If not, they lose their authority and fall into the dark well of insignificance.

The external world crashes in on us on waves of conflict, expectation, and doubt. It is on these shores that we learn to come to terms with the differences between the two worlds. David Whyte, in his poem "What I Must Tell Myself," says,

> When you are alone
> you must do anything
> to believe
> and when you are
> abandoned
> you must speak
> with everything
> you know
> and everything you are
> in order
> to belong.[7]

As leaders, we belong on these shores of conflict and must speak our truth and not become impotent victims in the maelstrom. Whyte does not mean we need to conform to belong. To belong we must be true to ourselves and take our place next to those who stand against the tide and not shrink from the strong seas of First World seductions. Our truth harkens us to belong to our principles and values, around which we are called to live.

Leaders accept people and conditions beyond their control or different than they would like them to be. Acceptance does not mean agreement—quite the contrary. It means that we don't curse the darkness, wring our hands, and simply complain, thereby frustrating ourselves, because those existing conditions will not change. Leaders see life as it is, not as they would like it to be.

Leaders with strength of heart contribute and participate; they do the right things, instead of just doing things right. Being in harmony with ourselves means sharing our ideas, thoughts, and talents with reverence for others and their own lives. Thoughts and ideas are powerful. They crush tanks and deflect missiles and can outwit "smart" bombs. Ideas are the basis for honorable efforts. The abstract ideals of liberty, justice, and freedom move the world because they ring in the very heart and soul of humanity.

Leaders are not driven by the ego needs of the First World—the need to do things for personal benefit and acclaim. They are driven by the reverence they have for the inherent value and goodness of human beings and the great potential human beings bring to this earth. They are stewards, which means they create the conditions necessary for people to meet their destiny and apply their talent.

Reverence is a form of stewardship. To be a good steward is to leave your home, relationships, community, organization, and world in better shape than you found them. To make that vital effort requires emotion and feeling. Passion and its sometimes-difficult cousin, intensity, can mobilize and inspire others. Diversion is not the strategy of leaders. The courage to face realities and to confront and even create conflict, to make a difference, is at the crux of leading.

Conflict exists in both worlds, but based on different terms. The conflict in our inner world is what we seldom mention, much less discuss. These conflicts are revealing and quite personal, and may swim against the tide of leadership myth. Inner conflicts determine our life's course and our character and humanity. They define us and help us examine our lives and the purpose we follow, often clarifying what we fear most in life.

Inside each of us is a longing. John O'Donohue, the Irish writer and poet, says, "Each one of us journeys alone to this world and it is our nature to seek out belonging." He states,

No one was created for isolation. When we become isolated, we are prone to being damaged; our minds lose their flexibility and natural kindness; we became vulnerable to fear and negativity. The sense of belonging keeps you in balance amidst the inner and outer immensities. The ancient and eternal values of human life—truth, unity, goodness, justice, beauty, and love are all statements of true belonging.[8]

The sense of longing we have as leaders is far different from the false images people have of the lonely, detached leader sitting on the top of the bureaucratic pyramid. Does it have to be lonely at the top? Isn't that a dysfunction that eventually causes leaders succumb to "fear and negativity"? Coming to grips with our natural desire for belonging as leaders and making positive connections is something we must confront—and maybe we need to help one another with those connections.

Deep within us is a longing to belong. Yet business schools and leadership programs promote detachment under the guise of objectivity. It is as if we believe that the more detached we are, the greater our mystique and the more respect we garner. This curious logic has its roots in the mythology of the leader as independent hero.

Part of our longing is to reach our calling, to live a life of significance, and to use our talents and energy to do what is good and right. Our calling lives in our spirit and haunts us when we follow a different road or steer off course.

We long to be connected in a meaningful way to the larger world. We all seek a sense of efficacy, a sense of being in our element. The German poet Rainer Maria Rilke describes the movement of the swan. He writes,

> This laboring through what is still undone
> as though, legs bound, we hobbled along the way,
> is like the awkward walking of the swan.
>
> And dying—to let go, no longer feel
> the solid ground we stand on every day—
> is like his anxious letting himself fall
>
> into the water, which receives him gently
> and which, as though with reverence and joy,
> draws back past him in streams on either side;
> while, infinitely silent and aware,
> in his full majesty and ever more
> indifferent, he condescends to glide.[9]

The swan in its element is a metaphor for grace. It speaks to being in your element, in the place you were meant to be. On land, swans lumber left and right and are the picture of pure awkwardness. But in the water, they move with unmatched grace and beauty. When we are in our element, we too are graceful, confident, and comfortable. Not everyone is cut out for the responsibility and obligations of leadership. People who choose leadership positions because of First World needs are swans awkwardly lumbering through the fields.

When we are where we are supposed to be, there is a grace about us and we find our voice and our place in the world. Then we live in dignity and with integrity. If our ego pushes us into places out of our element, then we lumber and weave. We are not a "natural." Our inner voice raises serious conflicts, and our happiness becomes the victim of our awkward, meandering walk.

Finally, inside each of us is fear. The fearless leader, another figment of our imagination, is a tribute to the facades people build and the protective masks they wear. Fear is a normal human emotion; the most fearsome images come from deep within us, not from the outside world. Even the great prophets of our world expressed fear: not fear from powerful physical forces and governments but of the fear from within.

In quiet moments we hold a mirror up to our life and compare the image to our deepest selves and longing. Many leaders fear not being up to the challenge. Many of us think we have "lucked out," and our talent and skill are not the reasons for our success. If you are ever placed on the sidelines of life, another fear is born: the fear of not being able to achieve your calling and doing what you were supposed to do with your life. The inability to contribute creates great fear. What bigger loss is there than not being able to use your talents and skill in the work you love?

Another fear is vulnerability. We fear that if we treat people in caring ways and honestly show them who we are as people, we will be perceived as soft and easily manipulated. Tough leaders want respect; they trivialize being loved under the rubric that if you are loved as a leader you either "gave away the store" or you are weak and softheaded. It is as if respect and love were incongruous and unnatural in the world of leadership.

Many leaders are attached to the role of leader and fear losing their title and position. This fear is dangerous because ultimately leaders do move on, by their own choice or others' suggestion. Facing attachments and qualms is essential in order for leaders to live peacefully inside without the growing cancer of anger or retribution.

The First World is laden with conflict. One major source of it is the illusion of control. People fight to gain control and they fight to maintain it. In a chaotic system like the universe, control is an illusion. The pages of our life flip at a pace independent of our wishes. Our lives hang on a thin thread of fate. Disequilibrium and the struggle for homeostasis are the natural order of things. The most we can hope for is order, which is no small achievement.

Control raises issues of power and pressure. Those who want control chase political, social, or economic power. Power, to them, is about the ability to direct events and other people's lives. They seek control over people, issues, and dynamics, sometimes for political gain or to obtain wealth and status. Our culture celebrates so-called barons of power and people of influence, as if they were immune to the vagaries and serendipity of life.

The search for power in the First World is a competitive one. Sometimes we compete with the system, trying to beat it and gain advantage. Other times the competition is over chasing the brass ring. In other cases, we compete with ourselves or with our parents. Today, many children face stiff competition, with their parents' economic and social status placing them under great pressure that can lead to alcohol and drug abuse, psychological disorders, or even suicide. Not meeting your own and other's expectations can be a grueling and unhappy experience.

These issues explode into dysfunction for individuals and for organizations as well. In the competitive environment of the First World, people try to be clever. They become gamesmen who try beating the system through deception in strategy or by parsing words. While being clever seems harmless—"stings" are a part of our culture and are pointed to as testament to American ingenuity—they can lead to more serious issues.

Corruption is the grandchild of cleverness. There are two types of corruption. One is painfully obvious in our society and business world. The contemporary view of corruption is bribery, money schemes, "cooking the books," false reporting, and selling inside information. This type of corruption is geared to First World advantage in worshipping at the altar of wealth and status based on a false definition of success. Unfortunately, many perceived leaders have feet of clay that taint their "success" because they use deception and smoke and mirrors.

> In the 21st Century great companies will figure out how to tap into people's hearts—their passion and their desire to make a difference through their work. Those companies that link passions to the generation of innovative ideas will have the capacity to sustain their growth for decades.
>
> —Bill George, former CEO, Medtronics, Inc.

Another type of corruption exists, yet it is one we seldom define. In fact, it is a classical view of corruption and has links to both the internal and external worlds. It has to do with calling, stewardship, and ego.

When leaders place personal good over the common good, that is corruption. In our society we do not have much discussion of the common good. We hear of entitlement and rights. We hear of every person for him- or herself. We hear that if you don't watch out for "number one," no one else will. These ideas are based on the notion that people are basically selfish. The common good or the commonweal seem like a value alien to our materialistic and ego-driven culture.

Leaders who are in a true sense stewards, and who operate from internal values and ideals, do not act in their self-interest at the expense of the common good. They look to what is good for all. They use their leadership position not to please power groups or themselves, but to take positions that help people see issues larger than their own parochial interests.

This classical view of corruption raises another issue: the conflict over purpose. What purpose drives our institutions and us? This question is one for both the inner and the outer worlds. It has to be answered by each of us individually, as well as by our society collectively.

The question of purpose has to do with justice, goodness, truth, beauty, equality, and liberty. Individuals seek liberty and freedom for themselves to pursue their passion and bliss. These noble ideals challenge us in what we want to accomplish as leaders. Almost all issues leaders confront have to do with one or more of these ideals. In pursuing them there is struggle—a noble struggle that involves high stakes and high risk. As Whyte says in "Sweet Darkness," "You must learn one thing. The world is made to be free in."[10] Whyte refers to freedom in the sense of being oneself—authentically—as an individual who wants to live a life of purpose.

Clashes and struggle are a part of life as we act on our yearnings and longing for noble principles. Conflict is not negative, because with it comes learning and satisfaction, creativity and innovation, and the application of human genius and wonder. Being true to our values in times of conflict is a venture of high order. We learn in these situations, gaining insight and understanding. Our errors are there for us to turn into nourishment for a better future.

Leaders have an obligation to engage people in a conversation. Leadership is about conversation. It is not paternal or maternal usurpation of people's options and reality. Through respectful and dignified conversation can come wisdom. A conversation is not a dispute or shouting match, as is so frequently found on cable television and radio today. A conversation is about commitment and passion and about the head, heart, and spirit of individuals. A formal way for leaders to have conversation is to engage in dialogue to achieve deep understanding through reflecting, clarifying values, and listening.

Bill Bradley, former senator, said that leaders should "say the things that everyone else is afraid to say. Ask the uncomfortable question. Tell your own story. Listen to the stories of others. That's leadership."[11] And when the burden is heavy and fears chase you in the quiet of the night, remember that peace can be found. Wendell Berry suggests:

> When despair for the world grows in me and I wake in the night at the least sound in fear of what my life and my children's lives may be, I go and lie down where the wood drake rests in his beauty on the water, and the great heron feeds.

I come into the peace of wild things who do not tax their lives with forethought or grief. I come into the presence of still water and I feel above me the day-blind stars waiting with their light. For a time I rest in the grace of the world, and am free.[12]

NOTES

1. "Simple Gifts" is a traditional Shaker hymn.

2. Woods, Nancy. *Spirit Walker*. New York: Doubleday, 1993, pp. 54–5.

3. Whyte, David. *House of Belonging*. Langley, WA: Many Rivers, 2002, p. 26.

4. Neruda, Pablo. *Extravagaria*. New York: Farrar, Straus and Giroux, 1974, p. 73.

5. "The Goal of Human Existence," excerpt from a radio broadcast on behalf of the United Jewish Appeal, November 4, 1943.

6. Havel, Vaclav. *Open Letters*. New York: Vintage, 1988, p. 153.

7. Whyte. *House of Belonging*, p. 14.

8. O'Donohue, John. *Eternal Echoes: Exploring Our Yearning to Belong*. New York: Cliff Street Books, 1999, p. xxiii.

9. Rilke, Rainer Maria. *The Selected Poetry of Rainier Maria Rilke*. New York: Vintage, 1989, p. 29.

10. Whyte. *House of Belonging*, p. 23.

11. Keynote address, "A Blueprint for a More Participatory Democracy," given on June 5, 1998, at the conference for Leadership for a New Century, Washington, DC.

12. Berry, Wendell. "The Peace of Wild Things," in *The Selected Poems of Wendell Berry*. Washington, DC: Counterpoint, 1998, p. 69.

3

Leadership and Illusions

The real change takes place within our souls; the real change takes place when the unfolding of our souls reflects in some deep, mysterious way the unfolding of the universe. Then it is—when an individual person dares to live within his or her truth—that the world is changed, forever.

—Vaclav Havel

Leadership is about life. It is about having an impact on others' lives, the life of the organization, and ultimately the leader's own existence. Life emerges in mystifying and engaging ways, pressing challenges into our faces and continually providing opportunities for finding meaning and living deeply. If our lives were flat lines with no peaks or valleys, leadership would not be necessary, and there would be little poetry in the nature of things.

Life is not a technical act of engineering that is lived by following a script or a manual. Life engages our total being and is unpredictable: it cannot be planned because our lives and destiny have plans enough for us. It is not simply about "doing," it is about who we are as a "being." It is poetic more than scientific. Leadership, like poetry, is about learning what it means to be fully human, to remember who we are, why we are here, and to find our place in the world.

Poetry and leadership seem to be odd bedfellows with very little connection. One seems so esoteric, and the other so grounded in the pragmatic demands of organizations. What does leadership have in common with poetry? Quite a lot, frankly.

Leaders and poets are charged with the same role, although their responsibilities and circumstances differ. They both place a perspective on life and its meaning, and turn the same soil of the human condition. They also try to engage people in conversation about relationships, what is important, and the meaning of life.

The metaphor of leader as poet is an important one, because metaphors establish a mindscape that affects the way we look at the world. The metaphors we have for leadership influence how we will act as leaders and how we think about leaders, who they are, and what they do. They set expectations and establish mental models.

How we observe the world is a product of our mind and how we think. We have pictures or mindscapes about the universe, and these mindscapes direct our awareness and insight—what we notice and what we ignore. Our language and thinking betray a great deal about how we perceive and think about life.

While we hold the world in our minds, seldom do we think about how we think. The Irish poet and writer John O'Donohue writes: "When you become aware of your thoughts and your particular style of thinking, you begin to see why your world is shaped the way it is."[1] There are dark sides and bright sides to this, however. We can become prisoners of our thoughts and our approach to or style of thinking. Our thinking can curb our creativity and restrict us from seeing in original ways. Conversely, we can liberate our perception by consciously reexamining the mindscapes that shape our thoughts; this helps us to see the world anew and discloses information we might have otherwise missed.

VIEWS OF LEADERSHIP

Scientific thinking has had a big influence on how we perceive our universe and our role as leaders. We create organizations that fit our ideas of how the greater universe works. If we perceive the world as a machine, then we become mechanics. If we see the world as an organic system, then we behave as gardeners. If we see the world technocratically, then poetry has little place in life, outside of being a pleasant diversion.

Old scientific thought from the 1600s, particularly Newtonian and Cartesian thinking, views the universe as a great machine, composed of parts, each designed for a unique function. The universe under this pattern of thought operates much the same as a clockwork that runs according to rational, linear logic. The assumption is that if you understand the parts, you understand the whole. A second assumption is one of control. If the universe is a contraption, then we gain control by finding the key gear, pinwheel, or lever that directs it.

Part-to-whole thinking is the basic foundation for solving problems and designing our organizations in this Newtonian mindscape. Think about it. The scientific method starts with breaking a "problem" into its component parts and then addressing each segment. Organizational bureaucracies are designed around the "problem" of producing work efficiently through the division of labor and the specialization of departments. Consequently, we talk of components, segments, departments, bureaus, or divisions—grades, levels, and groups.

Schools are organized like most bureaucracies. Children attend schools broken into levels, grades, departments, and subjects. They are sorted by chronological age, ability, or educational need. Education is divided into subjects, taught in units, and assessed in parts. If children pass all of the parts and meet the standards, it is assumed they will be educated people after thirteen years in public education.

Bureaucracies were born from the same mind frame. The irony is that Max Weber, the father of bureaucracy, developed the concept of bureaucratic structures as a reform to paternalistic organizations in which nepotism ran rampant. Bureaucracies were to honor talent and skill over patronage and nepotism, both of which infested 19th-century organizations. As the industrial revolution took hold and companies expanded and became bigger enterprises, specialized expertise became critical to success.

Specialization came into being, and the generalist faded as expertise, sometimes narrowly defined, filled departments and divisions. When work was diced into specialties, workers saw and understood only their portion of the job. Division of labor was the rule, and with it people frequently felt divorced from responsibility and accountability for the finished product. Workers were perceived as interchangeable cogs in the machine. How many times have you heard a leader say, "If only everyone did their part"? Rules, regulations, and job descriptions became an inherent part of all organizations in an effort to create uniformity of effort and productivity. Red tape and inefficiency became synonymous with bureaucracies, as organizational complexity became manifest.

In 1911, Frederick Taylor, a mechanical engineer, approached leadership scientifically, based on highly rational management techniques like time studies and efficiency analyses. Taylor's approach was a logical extension of the mindset of the world as mechanism. The famous Hawthorne studies on motivation took place during this efficiency-driven era that continued in the 1930s. Analyses of organizational components and operations were in vogue, used to find the one best way to get work done. Standardization of product and process were virtues, and systems and subsystems were put into place to ensure quality control. Increased productivity was the key goal.

After the scientific management trend, the human relations movement in the 1930s, 1940s, and 1950s focused on the worker, as a "component" that could be manipulated to ensure work was completed in a more productive and uniform manner. Satisfied workers, it was assumed, worked harder and were more cooperative with management. Motivation became an issue, and sociologists and organizational theorists studied the "organization man" and conformity. Job satisfaction studies abounded, as the administrators tried to find the links between motivation, satisfaction, and productivity.

Neoscientific management followed the human relations movement in the 1980s and 1990s and carried with it an accountability and efficiency focus, but with a greater emphasis on people. The motto "You inspect what you expect" came out of this era, and monitoring performance in a rational and objective manner was the order of the day. Participation and incentives, pay for performance, and bonuses were part of the movement to entice workers to produce more and meet concrete expectations. Leaders supervised and evaluated performance and were supposed to be objective and not betray feelings or emotions. They maintained an analytical and aloof posture. Management by objectives (MBO), complete with measurable and quantifiable benchmarks, frequently imposed from "downtown," was a key approach.

The MBO movement even affected our political life. During the war in Vietnam body count was the metric to determine our progress. If the U.S. military ran up a large "kill ratio" over the enemy, then, by all accounts at the time, we should have been victorious. Victory was defined by ratios and body counts, as if the intangibles of commitment and persistence were insignificant issues. They were overlooked because they could not be metrically factored into an equation. The loss in Vietnam defied the numbers and data. The planners and their statistical charts were wrong—victims of intangibles that rested in the hearts and minds of the soldiers. As Einstein said, "Not everything that counts can be counted, and not everything that can be counted counts."[2]

Scientific thought has captured us. We worship at the altar of science and scientific thinking. We reject or are skeptical of other ways of knowing, and accept science as the only valid approach to thinking and problem solving. Consequently, we build Newtonian walls of part-to-whole linear logic and construct a reality measured by quantifiable indicators.

> A leader's greatest obligation is to make possible an environment where people's minds and hearts can be inventive, brave, human, strong . . . where people aspire to change the world.
>
> —Carla Fiorina, former CEO, Hewlett-Packard

Leadership and management trends have adopted a "physics envy" approach. Clear cause and effect is sought, as we institute procedures to increase efficiency and effectiveness and a bottom line of units produced cost-effectively in a standard of time is the goal. School mastery tests are based on this approach, as students are to demonstrate proficiency and productivity of an established set of standards in a dictated period of time. Under this view, leadership is perceived as pushing buttons and pulling levers to get results.

The accent on process over people reduces the nobility of work to numbers and dehumanizes the very procedures that require human commitment. Getting the numbers becomes an obsession that may denigrate other important aspects of school and education. Instead of examining the "being" part of work and service, scientific approaches to leadership emphasize the "doings" of work.

Under scientific approaches leaders are supposed to be in control. If getting the numbers is critical, then leaders are the go-getters. They "make things happen" and are responsible, almost unilaterally, for the results and numbers. This assumption places the leader in the position of the all-knowing, all-responsible, all-important person in the organization. The lynchpin for success rests at the top of the hierarchical pyramid. The only real personality in the organization is the leader; everyone else becomes an interchangeable part. But it takes more than people "doing their part" to make a great, successful organization.

The poet Antonio Machado, in "Parables," provides a perspective on reason and its alter ego, the heart.

> Reason says:
> Let's seek the truth.
> The heart replies: What's the use?
> We already have the truth.
> Reason: Ah, to have the truth
> in one's grasp!
> The heart: What's the use?
> Truth is in hoping.
> Says reason: You lie.
> Comes the heart's reply:
> It's you that are lying, reason,
> saying things you don't believe.
> Reason: Between you and me
> there can be no understanding, heart.
> The heart: As to that, we'll see.[3]

To truly understand, we must move beyond the cognitive process of analysis and go to a deeper place, where thought is united with heart and spirit and wisdom. There are things we know that move our hearts, and there are things far greater in us that cause us to act in courageous and upright ways. Machado reveals that understanding may be a deeper thing than simply applying logic and reason. We "know" in several ways: cognitively, instinctively, and intuitively. We also gain understanding through our senses, including our intuition, which relies on all of our senses. In our hearts our inner voice—conscience—tells us what is right and good. Heartfelt expressions carry their own truth and have an impact far greater than logical debate.

> The three dimensions of leadership are mind, heart, and soul.
>
> —Klaus Schwab, chairman, World Economic Forum

The human spirit belies logic and science, and has produced great personal achievements when reason would dictate otherwise. There are multitudes of people who put themselves in jeopardy to save others or who were imprisoned in defense of an abstract principle. Seemingly superhuman accomplishments, such as the double amputee running across Canada and Lance Armstrong, a cancer victim, winning the Tour de France six times, demonstrate that the human heart and spirit defy reason. In doing so, these accomplishments lift all of us up in awe of human achievement and in inspiration.

Economists, with all of their forecasts, plans, charts, and graphs, cannot predict or account for the rise and fall of consumer confidence, which rides on emotional and nonrational perceptions and perspectives, and often does not respond to tweaks of interest rates, tax cuts, and other actions to get the economy moving. Serendipity is alive and well in the economy, often confounding the data-driven experts and their metrical analyses. Emotions and reactions cannot be calibrated with accuracy because people are more than brains and knowing is more than information.

Nonrational and inexplicable things happen in life and in organizations. Mistakes become huge victories. Unanticipated consequences squelch the best-laid plans. Forces are at play unseen by the rational eye. Leaders bump into these quirks of life, which are not accounted for in linear plans.

Sometimes, when we don't understand, we create illusions, which are based, in part, on how we desire the world to work, or are founded in speculation. As we search for understanding, we create mirages that seem logical and irrefutable but are pure figments of our imagination. These delusions can trigger behavior that can lead us astray.

LEADERSHIP AND ILLUSION

The illusions of leadership are embossed in the mythology of political, corporate, or community exploits. Mythology creates illusions, and illusions produce the leadership fantasies of heroic practice.

The mythology spawning these illusions is reflected in popular culture. From the Wild West to the streets of Dirty Harry's San Francisco, the American leadership icon is tough, controlled, and remarkably resourceful in going against the odds, all with a tinge of irreverent individualism. Illusions, however, plant seeds of frustration, since the world does not operate according to a script. Chaos, complexity, and coincidence can stymie corporate Bruce Willises and frustrate corporate Dirty Harrys.

Illusions are not reality. In fact, they can become dangerous because they can shield us from the truth and obscure our ability to learn.

Leaders who live wrapped in the veil of illusion are not able, then, to speak the truth. The fantasies we have about leadership not only deceive leaders but also establish unreasonable expectations for those who are led. These expectations often perpetuate a fantasy of the superpowered individual who unilaterally solves people's problems and, in a sense, makes them victims of their own impotence. The illusions below rob us of knowledge. The more common illusions include:

Illusion 1. The world is a logical place that succumbs to the power of logic.

Some leaders think Sir Isaac Newton is alive and well, because they adhere vehemently to the logic of part-to-whole thinking. The world with its playful, chaotic, self-organizing ways is immune to linear analysis. Even though it does not always respond to cause-and-effect action, there are patterns and connections in the universe. Fields are at work that cannot be seen or measured.

The polish poet Wislawa Szymborska has a stanza in the poem "The Turn of the Century" that depicts the unexpected nature of the universe.

> Already too much has happened
> that was not supposed to happen,
> and what was to come
> has yet to come.[4]

The unexpected nature of the universe wrecks havoc on forecasts and projections for the future. Future trends, based on data and scientific analysis, do not come to pass. Those things that no one thought of, or that were out of public consciousness, blossom with huge impact. Much happens that was not supposed to happen, and what was predicted to occur does not see the light of day. We are still waiting.

Many of the predictions and projections we make through the application of scientific methods, research, and tools fall short of reality. The unexpected happens and shows up on our doorstep, and what we plan crashes in the surprising turns of life. Life seldom plays out according to design—fate intervenes and unexpectedly colors our lives.

Chaotic systems are not predictable. With all the technology and science at their disposal, meteorologists still have trouble predicting weather. The world does not surrender to reason or to technology. Life intercedes, unforeseen things break our horizons, and science fiction becomes reality. Linear views of the world doom people to tinkering with procedures to produce better results, ignoring the fact that people cannot be programmed like software or behave in Pavlovian ways.

Illusion 2: Leaders, through control, make things happen.

In a Newtonian illusion, power and control make things happen. They are the cause of the intended effects—the way leaders drive change. This illusory power leads to command and authority structures designed to regulate workers by breaking work into manageable bits and pieces, and establishing and enforcing standard operating procedures.

Control is a mirage. If it were a reality, logic would rule, and the "levers of power" would work every time. Force can *move* people in the short term, but it does not *motivate* them. Power as domination can cause people to do things, but it controls them for only as long as the force is present. Even the most tyrannical governments do not have ultimate control over people, because no one can control thoughts. They can imprison our bodies, but our thoughts are free.

Leaders who scurry for control miss what makes organizations successful in a tumultuous world—order! Order grows from commitment to principle and provides direction and hope in tumultuous and muddled times. Order exists in a universe beyond our control. We can only react flexibly to circumstances and lose our omniscient fantasy of control.

Illusion 3: Important things can be quantified, measured, or benchmarked.

Scientific management reveres objective data and measurement. But not everything can be quantified. What quantifiable number can you place on creativity? Fairness? Imagination? Passion? Goodness? Caring? How do you quantify love or compassion? Yet these elements are important to successful schools, and they are the substance of our yearning. All are difficult to assess, but easier to feel and sense, usually over time or in the flash of a sensitive moment.

In "social" systems, logic does not always prevail. Feelings intercede. Destiny calls. Heart conquers mind. People wander off from the path of high-paying jobs and two BMWs to find something "meaningful" in their lives. The abstractions of justice, beauty, equality, truth, liberty, and goodness create waves of change as people sacrifice and, in some cases, give their lives for them.

Beware of those cemented to tangible proof, benchmark data, and tables of numbers. If they were right, the Edsel and New Coke would have been successes, and Truman would have been defeated in 1948. Subjective judgments, intuition, and hunches sometimes overcome the limitations of logic. People accomplish great things when conventional wisdom dictates otherwise. Leaders move beyond what is quantifiable and help people believe in the richness and poetry of the human spirit. Our imaginations and hearts lift us to great heights and new understandings, reflecting our basic goodness and spirit.

Illusion 4: Power is finite and should be hoarded.

Our society has an obsession about powerful people and is mesmerized by them. Some individuals thirst for power and want to hoard it, while others jump to grab "it" and try to keep "it." We behave as if power were a material commodity and possession. But what is power?

Historian James MacGregor Burns states, "At the root of bureaucratic conflict lies some kind of struggle for power and prestige. This struggle pervades the bureaucracy."[5] Max Weber believed power "enables a person to carry out his own will despite the protestations of others,"[6] emphasizing involuntary compliance, supremacy, and command. Ruling over others appears to be Weber's goal.

Typically power is associated with strength: to be powerful is to be strong and dominant. But Irish poet John O'Donohue says, "Frequently, people in power are not as strong as they might wish to appear. Many people who desperately hunger for power are weak. They seek power positions to compensate for their own fragility and vulnerability. A weak person in power can never be generous with power because they see questions or alternative possibilities as threatening their own supremacy and dominance."[7] First World impulses and ego drive people to gain a dominating position and feed their hunger for the illusion of control.

Another view of power exists that is different from domination. When electricians say "Turn on the power" they refer to energy. Leadership and energy are tightly coupled—creative energy, imaginative energy, collaborative energy. This "power" is at the root of successful people and organizations. Leaders energize, rather than dominate, people. Creative energy is unlimited if the conditions are there to nurture it. This power of energy is there to be shared and does not dissipate or need to be hoarded.

Illusion 5: Structure concerns roles, role expectations, and organizational charts.

Schools have been restructuring their "organizational charts" for years. In most cases, restructuring refers to how work gets done and how decisions are made. While organizational charts may be important, they do not trigger change if roles and procedures are built on bureaucratic control and authority relationships intended to control behavior and limit discretion.

What "structures" people's behavior when they are not at work? They don't have job descriptions or bosses in their personal lives. Administrative regulations, management procedures, and master contracts are nonexistent. Yet people are productive because they shape their lives based on a core of values and ethics, beliefs and principles, and ideas and philosophy—the "strange attractors" around which people act and make sense of the world.

The same is true in organizations. Companies that are tight around their values, beliefs, principles, and ethics but flexible around processes generate creative autonomy and organizational integrity. They have a sense of identity and produce energy and momentum.

Companies in existence for generations have a strong sense of values and a keen sense of self, according to Arie de Geus, former Dutch Shell Oil executive. He defines the concept of *introception*, which means that companies "must find their place in the world; they must develop a sense of relationship between their own persona's ethical priorities and the values in the surrounding world. . . . A living company is always engaged in questioning its own value system in relation to the ethics of the world in which it lives."[8] De Geus and poets have the same outlook and desire. Finding a place of belonging and making ourselves known are echoed in poetry, as well as in some corporate value statements.

Core values and ethics, which are essential in difficult times, are not mission or vision statements. They are like the basic tenets or creeds of a religion. According to de Geus, "in deeply troubled times when nobody knew the answer to totally new problems, the sharing of common values helped companies make choices to which individual employees could subscribe. They were sailing blindly into an uncertain future, but they could have confidence and belief in each other."[9]

Schools, in the churning, dark seas and heavy winds of uncertainty, confront complex problems, while politicians and others demand quick solutions. But quick fixes do not provide order in blistering times. Values and ethics, beliefs and principles, and ideas and philosophy pay dividends in commitment, creativity, and security in all times—good and bad. They fashion structure and define relationships and determine how decisions are made.

Illusion 6: Risk taking concerns decisions about programs, money, or political strategy.

We hear that leaders should be risk takers. There are hazards to proposing changes, allocating money, or traversing the slippery rocks of public policy. Risk taking, however, is more than proposing and disposing of programs or resources. Leaders who expose their values, ideas, and philosophy take a risk because it is personally self-revealing to have others witness your inner core.

Joseph Jaworski, author of *Synchronicity*, believes that leaders need an authentic presence—being open and passionate from the depths of their souls, allowing people to see who they are from their heads to their hearts. Having an authentic presence means connecting words with behavior and reducing the distance between leaders and others. Leaders must risk living their values in their relationships, openly sharing those values with others, and being true to them. Gandhi believed people should live truthfully, and that the level of "personal commitment in the search for truth will determine your commitment to truth in dealing with others."[10]

The risk of leadership is feeling vulnerable, exposed. Leaders fear removing the veil of hierarchical position and revealing themselves, because rejection cuts deep and personal, striking at the essence of one's true self and causing far more pain than the rebuff of a budget or program proposal. Authenticity takes courage because it calls for the risk of openly being yourself and revealing what you are passionate about.

Poets take the same risks as leaders. Through their writing, they expose their thoughts, ideals, and perceptions. Poets risk rejection by exposing what is in their hearts and souls. People who play the role of superintendent are trapped into following illusions about how leaders are supposed to "act." Leadership is not about "acting"; it is about "being"—being in relationships to others and being true to yourself.

IMPLICATIONS FOR LEADERS

Piercing these illusions means seeing the work of leaders with Marcel Proust's "new eyes." In doing so we must

- Recognize the world as a place of disequilibrium, chaos, and nonrationality that is also playful, self-organizing, and self-renewing.

> . . . in small matters trust the mind, in large ones the heart.
>
> —Sigmund Freud

Leaders deal with the chaotic world: that vast portion of life that does not respond to rational thinking, external control, or linear logic. Principled leaders help people get through the confusion of untenable times. People with clear and strong values and principles are powerful when facing adversity because they maintain integrity to their life's values and the ethics of their profession.

- Understand the intangible and invisible forces pervading organizations.

Intangible forces are at work in the web of our personal and professional relationships, creating fields that attract or repel people. For example, people committed to justice create a field, as do passionately loyal people pursuing a great cause. According to David Bohm, the British physicist, collective thinking is an intangible force that produces change through the power of its focus, synchronous events, or subconscious impact. Shared meaning and strong intentions coming from the flow of meaning can create change.

- Build strong connections and relationships between people that are essential for creativity, productivity, and commitment to surface.

Bureaucratic organizations separate people into roles and departments, building walls and artificial barriers. Information gets hoarded, mistrust develops, and the Plexiglas shield of status creates systems in which people see one another but cannot touch one another's imagination or hearts.

While everyone recognizes the import and impact of leaders, focusing strictly on them and their management styles does a disservice to other people in the organization. All of this can lead to disconnection and separation. The picture of the lonely leader at the top, struggling with monumental problems, is clichéd—and wrong. If it is lonely at the top, what is it like at the bottom? If there is nobility in work, then the leader's work is surely noble. But so is the work of everyone else. The notion that the higher up the hierarchy one sits the more righteous or important is one's work is demeaning to other people working in the organization. The existence of organizational haves and have-nots and the compartmentalization of people are destructive approaches that lead to disaffection and losing sight of the organization's mission.

The natural world is full of wonder and enchantment. We marvel at the relationships that exist in the natural world. Seasons unfold, and birds and other creatures, when in their element, thrive and act in accord with their destiny. The universe is an integral system.

Work should be wonderful too. Imagination and creativity certainly should exist in schools. Teachers, principals, and others work with the most captivating part of life—childhood. Reducing education to a scripted outline or a spreadsheet of numbers rips imagination from the classroom.

- Touch the heart and spirit, as well as the mind.

Great leaders attract people's hearts and intrigue their minds. They foster commitment when they demonstrate the full essence of what being human means, and recognize that relationships with others are all we have as we journey through life. People want human ties in their search for purpose and meaning. Physicists and poets understand that the fundamental nature of life is found in relationships.

In the poem "Three Goals," David Budbill offers a great perspective on the integral nature of relationships and the universe.

> The first goal is to see the thing itself
> in and for itself, see it simply and clearly
> for what it is.
> > No symbolism please.
>
> The second goal is to see each individual thing
> as unified, as one, with the other
> ten thousand things.
> > In this regard, a little wine helps a lot.
>
> The third goal is to grasp the first and the second goals,
> to see the universal and the particular
> simultaneously.
> > Regarding this one, call me when you get it.[11]

Budbill's humor is not misplaced. Being able to see the integral whole and the particular may just be the perspective that great leaders have. They see the dynamics and interrelatedness of forces and fields that affect people, issues, and organizations. They behave locally to have a global impact. This conceptual thinking and perspective is not always common, because some perceive small events, parts, and details and never make a connection to something larger. Others see tomorrow as a replica of today, without any change in dynamics, and others see the grand scheme of things—the whole—with all its complexity, mystery, and beauty. It takes more than a little wine to make connections, and certainly some people in leadership positions do not "get it." But those who do are said to have a vision and great anticipatory sight.

LEADERS AND POETS

Schools are living systems. They are creatures of the people who work in them, and as a result they do not surrender to the mechanics of management or engineering and technical approaches to leadership.

In living systems such as schools, growth is critical, especially in terms of the learning and capacity of people. Merging calling and meaning with the mission and purpose of schools is what people long for. In that regard, schools need caring, not curing. People cannot be fixed, but with care they can find efficacy and satisfaction in their work. They can become enchanted again with their talent and the purpose of the schools.

Natural systems are interrelated, and in them relationships are primary. Those relationships must be genuine and authentic, and respectful and sensitive. The miracle of life and the genius of human creativity are marvels to behold. Too often, the tangibles that can be measured are mundane and routine details of a more intricate mosaic. The genius of work often cannot be measured, because it comes from ideas, passion, energy, and thought.

Poets and leaders have the same calling, but in entirely different venues. Leaders work in the First World of pragmatic organizations and social and political systems, as well as the Second World. Poets work in the inner world, exploring the mystery and wonder of life in all its forms. In their work, both poets and leaders, however, have the same obligation.

First, poets tell the truth—and so should leaders. Poets help us face what life is all about, what it can be, and what it isn't. The role of leaders is to do the same. So often people think of leadership and public relations as going hand in hand. To some this means glossing over the truth or not telling the whole story. In putting poetry back into leadership, truth is essential. Without it, the dignity of those working with the leader is diminished, because falsehoods destroy relationships instead of building them.

Second, poets reveal a perspective that is missed or taken for granted. They put a new slant on the ordinary. Leaders do the same. Part of the attraction of work is to see the routine in a new light and appreciate the virtues of small things. Large programs do not always make a difference. Meaning is often found in being in harmony with the small things of life.

Third, poets see the world and life holistically, understanding the interconnections and dynamics, both subtle and obvious, that create reality. The hidden forces of life make a big difference; consequently, leaders must also see the integral whole and understand its dynamics. Otherwise they may manage details but neglect purpose.

Finally, leaders, like poets, address matters of the heart that make life worth living. Great leaders inspire the best in all of us; they understand the integral matters of the heart and the intangibles of spirit. Both are essential if commitment and meaning are to be tied to calling.

NOTES

1. O'Donohue. *Eternal Echoes*, p. 94.

2. Quotes of Albert Einstein. http://physics.augustana.edu/einstein.html, accessed September, 2004.

3. Machado, Antonio. *Selected Poems*, translated by Alan S. Trueblood. Cambridge, MA: Harvard University Press, 1982, p. 151.

4. Szymborska, Wislawa. *Miracle Fair*. Translated by Joanna Trzeciak. New York: Norton, 2001, p. 42.

5. Burns, James MacGregor. *Leadership*. New York: Harper Colophon, 1978, p. 299.

6. Burns. *Leadership*, p. 12.

7. O'Donohue, John. *Anam Cara: A Book of Celtic Wisdom*. New York: HarperCollins, 1997, p. 138.

8. de Geus, Arie. *The Living Company*. Boston, MA: Harvard Business School Press, 1997, p. 92.

9. de Geus. *The Living Company*, p. 108.

10. Nair, Keshavan. *A Higher Standard of Leadership*. San Francisco: Berrett-Koehler, 1994, p. 20.

11. Budbill, David. "Three Goals." In *Good Poems*, edited by Garrison Keillor. New York: Viking, 2002, p. 225.

4

Leadership and Relationships

> My continuing passion is to part a curtain, that invisible veil of indifference that falls between us and blinds us to each other's presence, each other's wonder, each other's human plight.
>
> —Eudora Welty

So frequently we hear that ours is a dog-eat-dog world in which only the fittest survive and no one can be trusted. We must protect ourselves—withdraw, stay aloof, and be on guard. This conventional wisdom flies in the face of how the entire universe operates and what leadership is really all about. Leadership is about connection—not separateness, suspicion, or distance.

Leadership concerns your relationship with yourself, with others, and with the circumstances you face in the world. Quantum physicists have found that all there is to reality is relationships—that the universe is a large network of interconnected relationships. So it is for leaders. Leaderships does not take place in a vacuum or in isolation. Leaders are in relationships on many different levels and planes.

A curious contradiction exists in organizations: people want a sense of connection, yet they describe relationships in terms of war metaphors. "Getting the troops ready," "capturing markets," "leading the charge," and "taking no prisoners" are phrases frequently heard. If what we think and say directs our behavior, then war metaphors focus us on a bunker mentality based on fear and control and getting ready for battle.

The problem, however, is that schools are not battlefields or competitive sporting events. They are places of growth and nurturing of mind, body, and spirit. Relationships in schools should be based on compassion, understanding, empathy, and forgiveness, not fear, reprisal, and allegorical death. Coordinating and creating relationships based on these notions requires passion and openness that bring people together in common purpose.

People want positive relationships that have virtue and wisdom. Unfortunately, these words are seldom heard in school environments today. Virtue concerns goodness, justice, fairness, and obligation. They are the primary ingredients in credibility and integrity. When leaders act without regard for principles—in behavior and processes—they lack integrity. Once it's gone, credibility evaporates, and then leaders cannot lead.

Wisdom is based on compassion, deep understanding, and insight. To be wise is to see moral and ethical principles clearly and to understand the interrelationships and connections in the universe and in life that bond processes, principles, and goals with consequences and integrity. Wisdom is creative intelligence that comes from the head and heart and that concerns the interconnected whole of life. Wise people see the subtle threads that make up the fabric of life and its network of relationships. They are astute and prudent in their reasoning and actions, and they are people who confront the sorrow and pain of life and understand the temporary and the lasting.

Leaders are expected to be wise and pursue truth and goodness in working with others in a positive, not an oppressive or repressive, way. The old myth that it is better to be feared than loved is extremely destructive. If you are not respected, the virus of revolution will attack organizational systems, sapping and squandering valuable creativity and commitment. Fear breeds contempt, not productivity and loyalty. People rebel against systems that are designed to drive and control them. People spend their energy and creativity to beat the system, and then the respect leaders desire becomes lost in struggle.

Thoughts color our perception of situations. If we think people are deceitful and the world is a sinister place, then our self-fulfilling prophecy will make it so. This does not mean that bad things do not happen. They do. As a leader what you think and how you react to the challenges presented to you and the people you lead are dependent on your perceptions. Acting on principle and optimism produces different results than acting on expediency and pessimism.

We need imagination to respond to what life offers. All of us are born with a creative imagination. When problems or the unexpected arise, opportunity blossoms, calling for improvisation and resourcefulness.

Life's complexity also calls for a sense of wonder about the texture, color, and revelations of life. Appreciating the beauty of life is an asset in participating fully in it. Leaders who see beauty in the unexpected and the challenges of life can help others adapt in vital and creative ways. Wonder breeds optimism, and optimism generates creative energy and enthusiasm.

RELATIONSHIPS AND COMPLEXITY

The world seems to move at a breakneck, hectic pace, and we are caught in trying to keep up and respond. Technology hasn't helped. In fact it may be a part of the problem, as people jump up from their stupor at meetings, responding to the jingle of their cell phones. We moved from two-day mail, to overnight express, to instant e-mail, and from months, weeks, days, and hours to nanoseconds.

As a result, mountains of data, tons of information, and hundreds of choices are at our disposal—all demanding a response, right now! As we seem awash in overwhelming complexity, we yearn for simpler times. In response, we lean on strategic and empirical approaches to find the magic key—the coordinates—that will unlock the secrets to success. We mine data. We try to find objective answers. We seek certainty.

In the process, we fragment our world, our problems, and ourselves into an increasing number of categories. Organizations are replete with "we-they" interactions—we sort people into those with us and those against us. We segment ourselves, when our natural inclination is to find togetherness and belonging as we try to find our place with others in this complicated world.

At the core is the issue of belonging in our personal and professional lives. A desire for belonging is reflected in wanting a sense of participation at work—a sense of efficacy and connection. Detachment is destructive, because people long to contribute and belong to something important. People do not necessarily desire "empowerment" to make decisions and determine processes. They desire a sense of efficacy that allows them to see their connection to others and their contribution to the greater whole. They seek happiness through pursuing a meaningful life and using their gifts.

We cannot find happiness through bureaucratic or mandated standards. Creating benchmarks, uniform expectations, and strategic goals does not always work in a world we cannot manage with certainty, much less precision. We live in an intricate ecology that is immune to directives, tactical initiatives, and power plays.

The surprises of life can create anxiety about the unknown and a fear of being left behind in isolation. Today our isolation can be self-imposed. Connectedness is a frame of mind that each of us must cultivate; otherwise we can get trapped by selfishness.

> Why are you so unhappy?
> Why are we so unhappy?
> Because everything you do
> And 99 percent of what you think
> Is for yourself.
> And there isn't one.[1]

Wu Wei addressed, in the 12th century, some of the maladies of 21st-century life. Happiness grows from altruistic motives, not selfish ones. Leaders who serve are not focused on themselves, because stewardship by definition is other-directed. Building relationships, even if it involves personal sacrifice or risk, is what memorable leaders and significant people have always done. Happiness is found in interactions and conversations with others. To find it, leaders must enter into a conversation about the worldly circumstances they face and work to find imaginative ways to respond.

Our thoughts also color the nature and depth of our conversations. Conversations are not one-way affairs. They depend on what each person uniquely brings to them and require a sense of stewardship and commitment rather than suspicion and fear. Conversations are important in relationships, and they are vital for leaders. Our lives are one long-term and engaging conversation with the world. To have credibility, that conversation with colleagues, the community, and ourselves must be honest and true to our principles and thoughts.

To converse while maintaining the integrity of our life's purpose and mission we need balance in our social, emotional, and philosophical lives. If we are out of balance, then we cannot be honest with ourselves or build relationships that are genuine. We depend on balance for judgment and clarity of focus if we are to have productive and supportive exchanges.

The irony is that in this high-tech world, our future success may rest on the old-fashioned, timeworn concept of conversation. If leaders do not create conversations, then organizations wither, lose their vitality, and eventually can die. So frequently we think of leaders charismatically rallying people through spellbinding speeches or taking unilateral action to solve a community's problems. If only it were that uncomplicated, we would simply have to teach prospective leaders rhetoric and oratory and a short course in analytical decision making.

The truth is people must come to grips with issues by thinking and talking about them over time. Conversation is essential for people to recognize issues, understand and solve them, and commit to action. Support comes only through understanding, which has its genesis in conversation.

Creating a conversation does not guarantee agreement, and it may even cause conflict, which is not negative if it spurs exchange about the right things. Conversation can lead to greater understanding of people's values and positions, and it may curtail the demagoguery and crassness that have been a part of public discourse in contemporary times, because in conversation respect and listening are essential.

> It is not what we learn in conversation that enriches us. It is the elation that comes of swift contact with tingling currents of thought.
>
> —Agnes Repplier

Conversation can also underscore confusion. Knowing what we are confused about is a gift, because when we face perplexity, we raise questions and seek answers. Confusion causes people to ponder and think—it stirs creativity and more dialogue and connections.

Margaret Wheatley extols the promise of conversation in her book *Turning to One Another*.[2] She indicates that in creating important conversations about issues people care about, several guidelines are important:

- Acknowledge and respect each other as equals and dissipate the superficial trappings of position and power.
- Curiosity is essential. Stay inquisitive about each other and the issue at hand. Question—ask "Why?" repeatedly, and listen.
- Recognize that we need each other's help to become better listeners and to find answers. Humility matters.
- Don't get trapped in producing "things"—products—when what should happen is patience to reflect and allow things to emerge. Even though life moves at warp speed, conversation is low-tech and requires time to think and reflect.
- Remember that conversation is a natural way for us to think together. Exchanging e-mails or debating or criticizing is not always thought provoking. Conversation with deeply embedded listening is critical to collective thought. Listening is the other and equally important side of communicating.
- Finally, conversation is "messy." It is not always efficient, and it may detour into the highways and byways of issues. Those side trips and diversions, however, may lead to the creative kernel that causes a breakthrough in understanding or finding a solution.

Most change starts from within, and as leaders engage in conversation with people, they can help their own internal transformation by following some simple ground rules.[3]

First, don't engage in conversation to win—that's a debate, not discourse. Leaders and managers frequently want to press their views and get their way, but in order to grow, we have to listen to learn. Take the time to fully understand the subtle issues at hand and not rush to judgment; ask what other people think in the course of a conversation and listen actively. As obvious as it seems, we need to seek out what other people think and have to say by bringing them into the conversation. Not everyone is aggressive in sharing ideas, and those who are more reserved may have the key to progress. Finally, when it is time to make a decision, use the insight gained from conversation and the intuitive energy to make it.

Conversation requires courageous speech that is honest and comes from our souls. When we speak from the heart, we speak with courage. When we speak with courage, we put ourselves, our very being, on the line, by showing our passion, sharing our feelings, expressing our fears, and defining our values. The cognitive rationale for decisions is easy to express in terms of costs and structures, but expressing the impact on individuals, relationships, and feelings takes courage. Sincerity comes from the heart and culminates in commitment.

Our journey as leaders is not one of isolation. Traveling together in communion and conversation is the road to true change. In these conversations, the shadows in the form of our fears, anxieties, and uncertainties are identified and diminished through the light of compassion and understanding. Change comes from the conviction and values that are outgrowths of our conversations with others and ourselves. We gain perspective.

John Shea writes:

> When we reach our limits, when our ordered worlds collapse, when we cannot enact our moral ideals, when we are disenchanted, it is then that we often enter into the awareness of mystery. Our dwelling within mystery is both menacing and promising. A relationship with exceeding darkness and undeserved light. In this situation with this awareness we do a distinctively human thing; we gather together and tell stories of God. We tell stories of God to calm our terror and hold our hope on high.[4]

Our stories tell of our dreams and aspirations, and are frequently tales of belonging.

Through conversation, we tell our stories—everyone has a story. And those stories have similar human themes. We might find that those with whom we disagree hold the same dreams for their children as we do for ours.

The world is made up of stories, not atoms.

—Muriel Rukeyser

BEING AND INTERCONNECTIVITY

As leaders we are supposed to "do things" to make a difference. The "doings" of leadership are spelled out in texts: planning, coordinating, analyzing, appraising, organizing, supervising, budgeting, delegating, and deciding, among others. Actually, all of these "doings" can be learned. There are different methods, techniques, and approaches, but the skill to do them can be learned rather easily. The relationships in the "doings" are the soft art of leadership—and cannot be mastered by reading a text. They involve a state of mind and a state of being.

The key, and most interesting, issue is that a person can be facile at the "doings" and still not be a successful leader. Certainly skill and technique are important, but of themselves they do not produce much over the long term. Systems for planning, organizing, and deciding are not immune to rigor mortis and decline. People find new methods and ways.

"Being" a leader is more than holding a title, sitting in the corner office, and "doing" systems. It embraces those things that make a leader authentic and genuine as an individual. After all, leaders are not wooden abstractions: they are real people who think, feel, and behave. "Being" is developing true relationships to others, to principles, and to ideas.

We are human beings, not human doings. Our "being" is our integral wholeness—mind, body, spirit, and soul. As beings, we are unique—we have a presence all our own, and no two of us are alike. We have distinct energy that can be seen and felt as part of our presence by letting what's inside of us come out, rather than externally posturing and positioning ourselves to win approval.

We talk of presence in leadership. Presence does not mean a dominating, overbearing, or arrogant demeanor: it speaks to being comfortable with ourselves and true to our principles. Leaders with presence are not fearful of not having all of the answers; they have calm confidence, and don't always have to control things. In reality we control very little—certainly very little of what is important in life. We have all seen fakes who backslap and posture, and we can feel in our guts the effects of "spinning" and insincerity. We can sense the lack of depth and hollowness in these actions—they are meaningless.

In our "being" we step back and ponder the meaning of things—raising questions and ethical and moral dimensions, and thinking about important matters. "Being" a leader involves much more than expertise and technical proficiency. We don't have to have an immediate response for everything.

Revealing ourselves—feelings, ideas, values, principles, and dreams—is an act of vulnerability. Unless people sense our humanness and approachability, we cannot connect with them. Brains are not enough, and ice-cold logic does not get people motivated. You may remember when presidential candidate Michael Dukakis replied to a hypothetical question about a physical attack on his wife. His reply just wasn't authentic and did not ring true. A coldly unemotional, analytical, and technical answer to a question about a situation like that seemed unnatural and artificial. Hence, he did not connect on the level that matters most—the human and emotional one. If we cannot connect with people, then we cannot use the talent, skills, and data they bring with them.

"Being" a leader requires that we openly seek answers, explore the tension between opposites, understand paradox, and suspend our inclination for certainty. Living life authentically requires letting go of the past that drains our energy or causes us to get stuck in former hurts. Leaders live in the present moment—not wallowing in the past, fighting yesterday's battles, harboring old ills, or fretting about tomorrow. "Being" involves tolerance, acceptance, listening, understanding, and humility. In "being," we find that the wonder of life may confound us, excite us, or throw us into an uncomfortable or surprising state. In these situations, leaders probe, step back, examine their responses, and uncover the meaning of what happened. Challenging assumptions, listening, and drawing out the facts and reasons behind events, not in an intimidating way, can lead to understanding. Without these efforts, the seeds of change fall on rocky ground.

Genuine leaders open themselves to experience and are reflective. As Socrates stated: "The unexamined life isn't worth living."[5] Leaders have self-knowledge, are comfortable in their own shoes, and are inquisitive and open to feedback. In the process of leading, we must also share our doubts. This goes against the idea of the all-knowing, confident leader at the helm, who always has a steady hand and an air of certainty.

Disclosing ourselves professionally is not a charade—clarifying our doubts as well as voicing our passion can lead to great credibility and honesty in our relationships. Genuineness speaks louder than posturing. Usually, when we are most insecure we try to position ourselves so people think otherwise.

Leaders do not always know how things are going to turn out. They are not supposed to discuss doubts because past mythology puts them in a cocoon of sureness. In some situations, particularly in crisis, some assurance is necessary, but even in these situations certainty is not expected—but optimism is. Over time facades of invulnerability and certainty become transparent and create loss of faith and cynicism.

Sharing our doubts and voicing our passions are risky because so much of us—who we are and want to be—is involved. Using open inquiry with the people we lead requires risk and assumes several things. First, when we disclose that we don't have all the answers, our hierarchical appendages dissolve and we can explore a mutually important issue with colleagues. This requires the skill of listening until we reach a common understanding of the values, options, and consequences of our collective reflection.

Secondly, "being" a leader assumes one important thing: that we have found our voice as professionals and as individuals. Voice is not about speech: it is about presenting and expressing ourselves honestly as we really are. Our voice is distinctively our own style, temperament, and presence. People accept it as a part of our character. Finding one's voice is no small thing, because it takes maturity, self-understanding, self-assurance, humility, and fervor. We know what we stand for, our purpose and principles are clear, and passion is followed with courage and honor. In a nutshell, we have defined who we are and we live with a sense of integrity regarding our life's values and calling. In finding our voice as leaders and professionals, we hope to find our collective voice as an organization and school.

Margaret Wheatley quotes Eudora Welty that the veil of indifference "blinds us to each other's presence, each other's wonder, each other's human plight."[6] This veil can fall on all of us, as we get involved in the "doings" of the day—completing tasks, planning strategies, interpreting data, budgeting, and meeting with a phalanx of people. We sometimes neglect the people and forget that our relationship with them is what is critical to success. We get mired in minutiae and can forget that we have obligations to the people with whom we interrelate.

Obligations are of a higher standard than responsibilities. There are moral overtones to obligations, and the commitment is greater. In a sense, we can fulfill the responsibilities in a job description and still not complete the work. A job is of lesser consequence than our work because work has to do with our calling, destiny, and hopes. We all search for meaning in life, and one way to find it is to discover our life's work and then meet our obligations in the pursuit to fulfill it. Our primary obligation is to the people we serve. When we meet this obligation we live with integrity.

Integrity is about virtue. In our society, we do not discuss virtue much; it has moral and spiritual overtones that deflect people from seeing how it applies to how we live and relate as leaders every day. Virtue has a lot to do with our connections to ourselves and to others and the energy and focus we bring to them. In a clear way, when we live a life of virtue, there is a sense of goodness in what we do—a moral drive based on positive principles and values. There is honesty in our words and behavior: they reflect each other. There are moral principles—respect, justice, fairness—that guide us and help us characterize our being, guide our words, and define our behavior.

When we live with virtue, we are upright and honorable in our goals, strategies, and conduct, even if it costs us our position, raises the hackles of people, does not meet the expectations of others, or creates controversy. When leaders live with virtue, they paint a profile in courage—they lead with boldness and conviction and their voice is heard.

LOVE, FEAR, AND FIELDS

Some of you are sitting there wondering what virtue and "being" have to do with leading a school district that exists in a complex social, political, economic, and cultural context. What does this have to do with schools and "business"?

In the best-selling 1990s business book *The Fifth Discipline*, Peter Senge discusses learning organizations. A person highlighted in the book is Bill O'Brien, former CEO of Hanover Insurance, who built a responsive, high-performing company and learning organization. And he did it by emphasizing virtue. O'Brien said in an interview:

> I had a deep frustration with the way large organizations hired people out of school, full of ideals and energy to make a contribution, and, because of bureaucracy and organizational politics, the vast majority of them became empty shells, counting the days to retirement. I didn't think it was a learning issue; it was more a virtue issue. I thought it was too much politics, too much kissing ass, too much lying, too much putting spin on everything. Really enormous doses of selfishness—not just at the top, but my department versus your department. I saw the infections in the corporation as inferior virtue. So I looked for the eternal truths or values that would elevate behavior above those lower things. . . . My bias is that companies have a big need for values and virtue, because that can turn on the entire workforce.[7]

Relationships, whether in public or private sector corporate life, must have virtue and clear values. Some fear that by approaching leadership from this standpoint, they will be perceived as weak and too idealistic for today's world. The real-life experience, however, of high-achieving corporations is not based on a foundation of greed and self-interest, or one of exploitation.

The word *love* never seems to be a part of leaders' vocabulary. Many would be embarrassed to use it, except to express love of children and family. We seldom hear it concerning the people with whom we work in pursuing our mutual passion, because it doesn't seem businesslike or doesn't fit with the rough-and-tumble image we have of leadership. However, all the great philosophers use love and its associated virtues as guides to a full, significant, and meaningful life—personally and professionally.

Bill O'Brien states:

> In America, we're trained to think of love as romance or family. But love is an act of the will. In business I believe love is helping other people complete themselves. When the events of life give a person responsibility where he or she has management over other people, a central part of that responsibility is: love thy neighbor, particularly those neighbors in your flock.[8]

The essence of leadership is to inspire people about their own competence and possibilities. When we love, we reach out and share ourselves with others and let them see our human side, our values, and our convictions. Love connects us to others, tying us together in a manner that is respectful, compassionate, caring, and emotional. Loving others allows us to accept and listen to them. As leaders, if we love the people with whom we work, we want them to fulfill themselves, to meet their fate, to use their talents to the fullest, to have a sense of efficacy, and to be connected to something bigger than their own self-interest. Helping others grow is an act of love.

Love also means that we try to understand each other, see the world from others' vantage points, and truly listen. Gandhi believed that love and courage are much more powerful than brute force, and by following that belief he changed a nation. He stated: "power based in love is a thousand times more effective and permanent than the one derived from fear of punishment."[9] Gandhi believed several things can destroy us:

> Wealth without work
> Pleasure without conscience
> Knowledge without character
> Commerce without morality
> Science without humanity
> Worship without sacrifice
> Politics without principle[10]

All of these are based on selfish motives, political control, and lack of virtue. Love for others and for oneself is essential in leading nobly, without using fear or suppression.

Fear, however, is prominent in the business world, in schools, and in other organizations, and it is dangerous—very dangerous—driving out love and destroying others. Leaders who lead through fear are doomed to failure over the long term. Those who are not trusted cannot challenge others to greatness because they diminish the potential of people and the organization. Fear builds barriers and walls, cuts us off from one another, and reduces adversaries to caricatures and demons. It stops conversation. The poem "In Silence," by Jorie Graham cogently reminds us of the silence that fear brings to the workplace:

> I try to hold my lie in mind
> my thinking one thing while feeling another.
> My being forced. Because the truth
> is a thing one is not permitted to say.[11]

Fearful people live in the silence of their own minds. They don't risk speaking their truth because no one can be trusted with it. After trust is overwhelmed by fear people will not contribute, feeling that their security is challenged. Insecurity creates a field of anxiety and silence that engulfs people, overwhelms their desire, and drives them into caves of silence.

Leadership can generate fields—some positive and others negative. What forces or fields, as a leader, do you want to pay heed to? What are your intentions as a leader?

In certain aspects of our lives we accept the presence of fields and invisible forces. That was not always the case. While Newton pondered gravity, he thought space was empty. Today we know there are forces at play in outer space and on this planet. We understand electrical fields, gravitational pull, and magnetic energy fields. Realizing that there are fields between people is harder for us to accept because of the hard-nosed idea that if we do not see them or cannot calibrate them, they do not exist.

Otto Scharmer, coauthor of *Presencing: Human Purpose and the Field of the Future*, has studied fields. He states:

> A field is, as every farmer knows, a living system—just as the earth is a living organism. I grew up on a farm in Northern Germany. One of the things my father . . . taught me was that the living quality of the soil is the most important thing in agriculture. Each field . . . has two aspects: the visible, which is what we see above the surface; and the invisible, which is what we find below the surface. The quality of the yield—the visible result—is a function of the quality of the soil, of those elements that are invisible to the eye. . . .
>
> The issue in working with social fields is that we haven't yet learned how to see below the surface, how to decipher the subtle structures and principles of the territory underneath. We haven't got the proper methods and tools yet that would allow us to dig beneath the surface to learn what otherwise would remain invisible. And, yet, every practitioner or experienced consultant knows, it is this invisible territory that is the most important when it comes to creating the conditions for high performance in teams, organizations, and larger ecologies.[12]

Invisible social fields do exist. They occur when our barriers drop and we get into a different "plane," while working on a project when concentration is intense, when our vision becomes more acute and things come easy. Time flies in the jet stream. We seem in harmony with the universe and with others, and there is a sense of flow. We feel in the "zone."

We can feel social fields as they engulf us during holidays, when everyone seems in sync and there is a sense of warmth and openness. They are also evident in crises, when people feel a sense of obligation, compassion, and intense connectedness to one another. In crises, work gets completed without leaders asking. People share, barriers drop, and people are joined in their common humanity.

Roger Salient, former Ford Motor company executive and CEO of Plug Power, a fuel cell company, has seen fields in all aspects of his life, including the workplace. With fields,

> there is a feeling of working together, a symbiotic relationship. There is an intimacy that has meaning to them as well as me. A kind of flow exists between us.

Every now and then I experience this kind of field in the workplace. Every action, every note is in the right place, and it all becomes a symphony. When I leave that moment, when I walk out of the room, the feeling lingers. It is as if I've been bathed, and I feel refreshed.

When you're in that kind of field, it's as though you've walked into a fog that's alive and all the rest of the world disappears. The fog is the medium of interconnection between you and other living creatures. It is like being in a swarm of bees. There is no orientation, no real north. There is no time.[13]

Fields happen, it seems, by chance. In organizations, fields can be established through thought and values that are articulated, discussed, and, most importantly, lived. Thought and values unite people in a common cause and establish links to what is meaningful. Physicist David Bohm believes thought is a system connecting people and establishing a collective mood or aura of concentration, perception, emotion, or commitment—a field. Hence the power of collective thinking can bring great breakthroughs and cause intention to become reality.

In creative organizations, you can sense the field. When people say they can "feel" the climate in a school or organization, they are sensing a field. Creative people go with the flow, help things emerge, and see things in unique ways. When people are creative a field surrounds them in their pursuit. People and the universe become woven together by a fabric of invisible connections.

Three principles direct us in our pursuits and affect the nature and direction of our relationships.[14] First, there is a "shift of mind" when we see the world as full of possibilities. In our relationships with ourselves and others, we can get stuck in what is and adopt a cynical view that nothing ever changes or that there is only one way to do things. Artists and other creative people see the world anew and as an open possibility. It is not static; it constantly evolves, just as our lives do. The images inside our being help us make sense of the world. The question is: What are those images?

Secondly, we find meaning when we see ourselves as part of what is unfolding. We define ourselves in relationship to the world, to others, and to the phases of our lives. Being a part of a creative activity involves our relationship to the issue, to our perspective of the world, and to others. If we are closed to the world and to others, then we cut ourselves off from connecting with what can emerge in our world.

Being engaged in something that is meaningful and creative requires deep commitment. We can see that commitment in the early aviators who bucked the odds and flew when people said they couldn't, the astronauts who went to the moon when skeptics over the centuries could only dream about it, the pacifists who freed a country from imperialism through nonviolence when detractors said it wouldn't work. Commitment to meaning is profound and energizing. We would give up our lives rather than surrender that pursuit because we find our relationship to the world meaningful to our own life.

While we're connected through our relationships, we also need space for the fire of creativity to burn. Judy Sorum Brown captures that notion in her poem "Fire":

> What makes a fire burn
> is the space between the logs,
> a breathing space.
> Too much of a good thing,
> too many logs
> packed in too tight
> can douse the flames,
> almost as surely
> as a pail of water would.
>
> So building fires
> requires attention
> to the spaces in between,
> as much as to the wood.
> When we are able to build
> open spaces
> in the same way
> we have learned
> to pile on the logs,
> then we can come to see how
> it is fuel, and the absence of fuel
> together, that make fire possible.
>
> We only need to lay a log
> lightly from time to time.
> A fire
> grows
> simply because the space is there,
> with openings
> in which the flame
> that knows just how it wants to burn
> can find its way.[15]

Reflection is a meeting with yourself. We need to go off into the metaphorical woods of solitude and think. Here we can heal our doubts and reflect on how we connect to the other "logs" in the process and study the flame of creativity. This "space" can generate large and more nourishing flames. However, if we get too close, we can be burned by groupthink or find issues of ego scorching our souls. In the emergence of creative ideas, space and silence are very important.

The space between people in this context is not aloofness or a matter of power. Space feeds the flame to tap into ourselves and to synthesize and intuit approaches that may provide vital creative oxygen to others. Sometimes, the person who goes off to his or her own mountaintop and howls in the wilderness has the essential insight that finds the spark that ignites energy, warmth, and inspiration in others.

These flames produce a creative "field" in which barriers plummet, intuition and reason are active, and people are tightly focused and engaged in listening, understanding, and encouraging the emergence of something new. Packing in too close, or adding more logs, may not be productive. Relationships in a creative endeavor need the both closeness to engage and solitude to reflect.

Time is also necessary for reflection to take place, and the group may need collective solitude to get off by itself away from the humdrum nature of daily events. There is an art to finding that balance, and leaders understand how to provide the time and environment necessary for ideas to grow and develop.

RELATIONSHIPS AND CONFLICT

Interdependence pushes us to examine our responsibilities and obligations to others and the greater community. Communities and society need people who are self-sufficient but who also recognize the fact that they are not islands unto themselves: that others need them and they have an obligation that extends beyond egocentric interests to meet their obligations as members of society.

Values and commitment are the glue that makes learning communities thrive. Learning is powerful because it provides people with the opportunity to give something back to the people who helped them and to those who are needy, as well as to improve their communities.

Individuals can have an impact and, indeed, are obligated to use their education in responsible ways. Leaders help people move from dependence to independence to interdependence, with a sense of social and personal responsibility and obligation. Only then does our society become composed of communities of common interest with strong coherence and vision.

In this vein, leading is not a Pollyanna practice in which everyone is happy and always following the leader, without question, and with total acceptance. There is conflict, and conflict can be painful. In conflict, however, we have choices. As Heraclitus stated:

Your soul is dyed with the color of your thoughts. Think only those things that are consistent with your principles and that can stand the brightest light of day. The content of your character is your choice. Day after day, what you choose, what you think, and what you do make you who you are. Your integrity is your destiny . . . is the light that guides your way.[16]

Being interconnected causes us to bump into one another over ideas, ego, and passion. We can be fearful, offended, or hurt in the process. In conflict, we have a decision to make, a choice as to how we approach the issue. Our choice is in how we respond—with integrity or by protecting our First World attachments.

Conflicts come up in a number of ways, according to Fred Kofman.[17] This conflict may arise at work or in our personal lives. Conflict surfaces when

- we force ourselves to do something painful;
- we force others to do what they do not want to do;
- we force each other to do what neither wants to do;
- the other person wants to do something we don't want them to do.

In these situations, our ire and frustration can be raised, or we may feel pressure from other sources, as we require people to do things they resist. Causing this conflict may be necessary, however, to do the right thing.

In any case, we have a choice and so do the others. The choice comes down to either being a victim or being a player, not in a manipulative manner, but in the sense that we take responsibility to respond to the circumstances producing the conflict.

Victim or player? What are you? What should leaders be?

Our society is obsessed with victimhood. It seems that no one is responsible for anything, as people are reticent to accept their obligations in difficult situations. People run for cover. They send "cover your ass" memos and make excuses. No one takes responsibility for a bad situation, and even fewer accept the obligation to do something about it.

Fear is a part of being a victim. Adopting a victimized stance has its genesis in the fear of facing disapproval from others—the citizens, the staff, the school board, or others. Conflict can cause embarrassments, and as leaders, all of us fear public humiliation because of the visibility of our position. Confronting conflict or failure is a threat to our egos and self-esteem. Facing failure and conflict in a straightforward manner takes courage and confidence. Leaders who always make excuses in the face of failure or deflect responsibility and blame others soon lose their standing.

> In the arena of human life the honors and rewards fall to those who show their qualities in action.
>
> —Aristotle

Victimhood is a relatively comfortable position because victims avoid and deflect any responsibility for the situation. They cite being adrift on the winds of fate and external circumstances or past situations. They linger in the fog of the past and feel impotent in the present. Things are beyond their control, and, as a result, victims are comfortable criticizing and blaming others, while accepting no responsibility. Excuses are prevalent.

In a curious way, victims maintain their self-esteem in the face of problems. If things are beyond their control and they are helpless and powerless to respond, then they are not responsible and they are innocent of any culpability. Children frequently resort to victim behavior when things go wrong. The old saw "The dog ate my homework" is indicative of being powerless. The logic of victimhood deflects criticism; things are beyond victims' control, and they cannot act in response.

The results of acting like a victim are anger, resentment, resignation, and bitterness. If you think like a victim, then you live like one. Sure, life is difficult and bad things happen. People die. Natural disasters happen. New regulations are passed that impair autonomy. Citizens vote against the budget or construction project. Things do not go our way. It is easy to feel victimized and retreat or throw up our hands in frustration.

Players approach the situation differently by accepting the events and going forward according to their values and principles. They have the capacity to use their free will to respond and get involved. They live in the present and react to the conflict positively and responsibly. Players look forward, not backward, and they actively participate and contribute in difficult situations. They have a sense of self-worth.

Players make the conscious choice to be "response-able". They are "able" to use their free will and autonomy to respond. Leadership is not always necessary when things are moving along well. We look for leadership in tough times and when things are out of control. While not controlling fate, leaders are players who can help create order and respond to situations with mindfulness and optimism. Even if we are being fired unfairly, we are "response-able" to leave the job on our terms by preserving our principles and dignity.

Players protect their integrity by acting in accordance with ideals and creating a dialogue around the issue or conflict. They accept the responsibility to live on the bubble and engage in living life—in the moment, as an active participant. Accepting responsibility, however, carries with it accountability.

Accountability is the other side of responsibility. When you use your free will, you are compelled to be accountable. If we take charge as active players in situations, we must explain our behavior and actions. We are accountable for outcomes and for the processes we use to achieve them. If we do not want to be accountable, we do not make choices, and we continue to live in a state of suspended adolescence. If you can't stand the heat of being "response-able," sit with the victims.

LEADERS, ATTACHMENTS, AND LEADERSHIP

Gandhi believed that all leaders must know their attachments; otherwise they will succumb to them in subtle ways that compromise their principles. Attachments are "relationships, possessions, privileges, and other components of our life we do not want to give up."[18] Knowing yourself as a leader means knowing your attachments.

Leaders can be attached professionally to competence, status, power, and acceptance, among other things. On a personal level, they can be attached to status, money, geography, or possessions. Some attachments are conscious ones, and others are subconscious. Discovering attachments, however, is essential; otherwise they can cloud leaders' judgment.

Attachments to power, privilege, and possessions can make integrity with regard to principles difficult. They can create subtle confrontations within us. Do we risk jeopardizing an attachment to do the right thing? For example, many leaders are attached to competence—being perceived by others as capable and assured. Competence is demonstrated by success, and success leads to security. Some leaders and executives cannot admit to a mistake or indicate a shortfall in reaching goals because of their attachment to competence. To do so jeopardizes their attachments. Failure is anathema to people who always have to be right and recognized as successful. Their self-image is tied to perceived triumph.

Competence, success, and security are positive things in life. The issue is attachment. For example, if the data indicate that goals are not being reached and a leader's self-esteem or job security is threatened, will he or she speak out and candidly report the shortfall, or will the attachment to competence and security overrule reporting failure? There are examples in all sectors of life of data being stretched, false pictures being painted, issues being buried, or scapegoats being identified to protect a leader's image.

People in danger of losing their power and authority sometimes compromise principles and fall into self-protection, secrecy, or blaming, resulting in obscured judgment and focus. Attachments are challenged at the crossroads where the soft issues of leadership—compassion, credibility, forgiveness, and integrity—meet the hard data and information that are indicators of achievement and success.

Fred Kofman's comments about leadership and attachments define this dilemma. He cites the Baghavad Gita: "the wise man is free from all attachments."[19] Being free of attachments does not mean being free from caring and working on behalf of positive virtues and principles. It does signify not putting ego or other self-directed desires in the way of larger issues. Being free of attachments liberates leaders from having subtle self-interest compromise main principles. The risk is that leaders can fail; but that failure should not be due to fear or self-interest.

Wise leaders free themselves from their attachments and become at peace with what results from their best efforts. Since we live in a world of disequilibrium, there are forces—manifest and hidden—over which leaders have very little control. Those forces, plus the best-intentioned and -planned initiatives or strategies, can lead to failure or falling short of expectations.

Being at peace with success or failure is not easy and does not imply that failure is accepted. We must simply be at peace in making our best efforts. In that regard, reporting problems is in the best interests of the organization and the children. It is an act of courageous leadership, not an act of weakness or incompetence.

Principles are not always tangible; they can be abstractions that are always in the process of being defined by events. For example, is it ever appropriate for a leader to lie, or does lying compromise integrity? Some might say that the President of the United States cannot always be truthful in order to protect national security and our democracy. But others, Gandhi included, would argue that a president who lies weakens the very democracy he or she intends to protect, because the people become untrustworthy of and cynical toward a government that does not tell the truth. Credibility vanishes, and with it the ability to lead. We lose the very thing we try to protect through deception.

A leader's moral obligation is to not subordinate principles to attachments or the desire for success. Virtue comes from adherence to principles in pursuit of success. That means that data and information are managed, analyzed, synthesized, evaluated, and presented honestly and ethically even if they jeopardize a leader's personal standing and attachments.

If failure occurs, then the leader, organization, and community can continue to learn and search for the right answers. No one can succeed all the time. Falling short offers the opportunity not only for growth, but also for creative problem solving, learning, and deepened commitment.

LEADERS, RELATIONSHIPS, AND FORGIVENESS

Relationships are made of gossamer wings—they are fragile and sensitive. Leaders build, stimulate, and nurture them, or they can neglect, abuse, or destroy them. Relationships are connected or broken, fluid or rigid, trusting or suspicious, close or distant, formal or informal. Leaders either erect bridges or create walls; they open or close relationships. Leaders have several different relationships, all requiring ethical and moral care.

A primary relationship for leaders is the one they have to themselves and the kind of leader they want to be. They must determine what is authentic, genuine, and true to who they are. Leading with integrity with regard to one's inner core is the key to authenticity.

Another relationship is to others: the children and other professionals and the people in the community. Do these relationships bind people together or do they segment and Balkanize them? Is the whole greater than the sum of the parts, or vice versa? Knowing whether relationships are built on trust and compassion or suspicion and control is essential in answering these questions.

Finally, a third relationship concerns stewardship—bringing about the best for the schools and making them better than they were is being a steward. Which acts enhance and heal the organization and community, and which ones place them in jeopardy? Some relationships build capacity in an organization and others destroy talent and potential, depleting energy and strength.

Conflict, as well as joy and excitement, is a part of all of these relationships. Sometimes conflict is aggressive and other times it walks on the velvet slippers of change and innovation. But it can create tension, misunderstandings, hard feelings, confrontation, and anger. Negative conflict can cost leaders their credibility and their personal and professional relationships.

In this context, the need for forgiveness and healing displays itself on a daily basis. Hostility snaps the calm of school classrooms. Conflict takes its toll in labor-management disputes, and rancor unsettles the policy boardrooms of school districts. Conflict causes pain and often loss, whether of life, wealth, or efficacy. Fragmentation occurs, rupturing relationships. Disconnects happen. Disruption appears. And people become imbalanced, tentative, and unsure.

Leaders face these difficult issues. In this environment, they can get hurt, offended, irritated, deflated, disappointed, infuriated, and even depressed. In the tough-talking mythology of leadership, the quote "I don't get angry, I get even" has become clichéd. But getting even requires retribution and all the negative energy it carries. Scapegoating, stereotyping, dehumanizing, and blaming all set the stage for retaliation, which builds barriers and frequently results in a continuous cycle of active or passive aggression.

To lead, one must forgive, and forgiveness requires a big risk. Contemporary leadership literature espouses the view that leaders should be risk takers. But the risks are not defined. One of the largest risks for leaders is the act of forgiveness. Forgiveness, whether in our personal or professional life, takes strength and courage, and healing seems so benign and soft—far from the flurry of flags or saber-rattling bravado. The courage to forgive, however, may be the catalyst that unleashes talent and energy for organizations and helps people to meet their full potential and find balance.

Former secretary of defense Robert McNamara in the documentary *The Fog of War* said that to keep out of military quagmires we have to follow one rule: have empathy for our adversaries. Empathy and compassion are two ingredients in a caring relationship. But our first inclination is to fear our enemy, not have empathy or see the world from his or her perspective. Empathy is being sensitive to the experiences and thoughts of others.

Gandhi understands the importance of forgiveness. "The weak never forgive. Forgiveness is an attribute of the strong."[20] The irony in our society is that striking back and seeking retribution are perceived as bold leadership. The healing act of forgiving is frequently a magnet for derision and mockery, and often it is falsely perceived as an act of weakness. Forgiveness is often misunderstood because it is confused with condoning, approving, disregarding, or excusing actions and behavior.

Forgiveness, however, is about recognizing conditions as they are, complete with all the hurt, disgust, and anger, and moving beyond current circumstances—releasing the past so healing can take place. Leaders can lead based on the principles and values that appeal to the best in us rather than succumb to the dark side of human nature, filled with evening scores, harvesting pounds of flesh, or pursuing vendettas. Forgiving is moving on.

Forgiveness in this context is ethical forgiveness, not theological forgiveness. It is based on one human being forgiving another, and not the theological view of forgiveness by a deity or higher being.

Ethical forgiveness involves five things. First, forgiveness involves wholeness—bringing things together and fulfilling a sense of integrity between individuals within the organization. Wholeness involves mending breaches, uniting fragments, and creating a sense of oneness and connection.

Second, forgiveness requires a sense of inner balance and peace. A person who seeks revenge and retribution is not at peace. The turmoil of the conflict and resulting hurt can preoccupy a person's life, coloring his or her priorities and relationships with others. Peace comes with balance, optimism, and confidence that there is a better future. Peace is a reciprocal result of forgiveness and is related to the third characteristic—release.

Release means to accept the situation and move into the future. Seeking revenge allows the emotions and hurt of past actions dictate future ones.

Leaders do not live in the past; they have a vision of the future and act to construct bridges to better times. They do not live behind the walls of what went before, and they do not live with illusions and paranoia. Forgiving means living in the moment, looking to the future, and not getting mired in what went before.

Fourth, forgiveness generates openness in relationships by removing the debris and segmentation of what went before. Forgiveness eliminates obstacles and reestablishes broken or disabled connections in communication, understanding, and emotion. It eliminates the organizational cancers of scapegoating and blaming that are so pervasive in dysfunctional workplaces. These cancers are indicative of organizations that need forgiveness in leadership.

Finally, to forgive is to heal, which means that the organization retains and recaptures its integrity of purpose and principle in its relationships and operation. Without forgiveness, healing cannot occur. Instead, the hurt from the conflict festers and the organization loses its strength and energy. A healed organization becomes whole again—with healthy, genuine relationships rooted in integrity and noble principles.

Organizations cannot function if they are fragmented and reliving past hurts as the rest of the world moves on. If they do relive past hurts, they become corrupted. Leadership recognizes the steps necessary to move schools into the future and to build performance capacity so schools can be successful.

Leadership has an ethical and moral center. Ethics are directed at relationships, enhancing them in positive ways and working to fulfill their potential and enhance their creativity. Forgiveness is a creative act—and act of construction, not destruction. It re-creates and renews the connections between people, sometimes in new and different terms. The energy and understanding in these relationships is changed. As an act of love and not anger or disdain, forgiveness can transform and heal.

There are several compelling reasons for superintendents to act in forgiving ways:

- Integrity: Forgiveness is the foundation of what is good within us. The ability to live with integrity based on our ethical and governing principles requires us to forgive and live in the present moment so we can face the future. Forgiveness allows healing. All religions and philosophies view forgiveness as a high human virtue that ennobles and transforms.
- Relationships: Reality is grounded in relationships. And relationships require people to forgive in both personal and professional environments. We cannot collaborate or cooperate without the ability to forgive. Forgiveness creates positive interactions and builds dignity, respect, and affection that cannot exist in a ruthless and compassionless environment. Fractured or disabled relationships lead to isolation,

anger, and illusion—all of which reduce the organization's ability to operate at optimum levels.

- Talent and Capacity: To use their full talent and potential, people need to feel a sense of efficacy, which requires a sense of wholeness and connection. Increasing the school's capacity as a learning organization compels us to move beyond the intensity and emotions of conflict in order to fulfill our purpose. Forgiveness lights the pathway to potential and the future. Creativity does not exist in an environment that is judgmental, callous, or vindictive.
- Transformation: The literature is full of references to transformational leadership, but often does not define what the transformation is. Transformation compels forgiving others who may have been angering and irritating during the conflict of change. Before leaders can help transform their organizations, they need to transform themselves. Forgiveness transforms attitudes and relationships.

As leaders, we must forgive ourselves for making mistakes and falling short. We must do this before we can engage in helping the organization forgive on a broader scale. To be effective, leaders need balance, and to be in balance requires forgiveness.

In conflict the soil can get poisoned unless leaders lead the way in forgiving. An eye for an eye can only lead to escalated clashes, deeper damage, and losses in organizational potential. People's lives become broken and unfulfilled.

Leadership "in relationship" to others requires moving beyond tolerance to forgiveness. "Being" in distress, "being" in the past, "being" angry, and "being" in a vendetta are destructive acts personally and organizationally. Settling scores does not appeal to the best in us.

The great leaders of the past centuries forgave and took the ultimate risk of doing what was right, not what was popular. We can learn from Gandhi, King, Eleanor Roosevelt, Marshall, Truman, Ford, Lincoln, Tutu, Mandela, Havel, and from those who forgave us. They transformed the world through forgiveness.

NOTES

1. Wu Wei, as quoted in Senge, Peter, Joseph Jaworski, C. Otto Scharmer, and Betty Sue Flowers. *Presence: Human Purpose and the Field of the Future.* Cambridge: Society for Organizational Learning, 2004, p. 190.

2. Wheatley, Margaret. *Turning to One Another.* San Francisco: Berrett-Koehler, 2002.

3. O'Brien, Bill. "Twenty Years of Organizational Learning and Ethics at Hanover Insurance: Interviews with Bill O'Brien." By Barry Sugarman. *Reflections,* Society for Organizational Learning, vol. 3., no.1, 12.

4. Shea, John. *Stories of God: An Unauthorized Biography*. Chicago: Thomas More Press, 1977.

5. Socrates. www.philosophypages.com/hy/2d.html, accessed September, 2004.

6. Eudora Welty, quoted in Margaret Wheatley. "Servant Leadership—Community in the 21st Century." Speech, June 1999, Robert K. Greenleaf Center for Servant Leadership.

7. O'Brien. "Twenty Years," p. 8.

8. Jaworski, Joseph. "The Heart of True Leadership," Hamilton, MA: Center for Generative Leadership, p. 12.

9. Gandhi, Mohandas K. www.gandhi.ca/gandhi/quotes/power.php, acccessed August, 2004.

10. Gandhi, Mohandas K. www.mkgandhi.org/mgmnt.ht, accessed October, 2005.

11. Graham, Jorie. "In Silence," in *Never: Poems*. New York: Ecco, 2002, p. 12.

12. Senge et al., *Presence*, p. 109.

13. Salient, Roger. "Interview with Roger Salient." By Susan Szpakowski, in *Fields of Connection*, Shambhala Institute, January 2004.

14. Jaworski, Joseph. "Conversation with Joseph Jaworski." Cambridge, MA: Society for Organizational Learning, October 29, 1999.

15. Brown, Judy Sorum. "Fire," in *The Sea Accepts All Rivers and Other Poems*. Alexandria, VA: Miles River Press, 2000, p. 27.

16. Heraclitus. Quoted in Kofman, Fred. *Unconditional Responsibility*, a paper published by www.axialent.com, September, 2001, p. 2.

17. Kofman, Fred. Speech at the conference "Spirituality and Leadership," Shambhala Institute, 2001.

18. Nair, Keshavan. *A Higher Standard of Leadership*. San Francisco: Berrett-Koehler, 1994, p. 37.

19. The Baghavad Gita, translated by Stephen Mitchell, as quoted in Kofman, Fred. *Unconditional Responsibility*, a paper published by www.axialent.com, September, 2001, p. 7.

20. Gandhi. www.angelfire.com/de2/quotes.html, accessed August, 2004.

5

Leadership and the Mirror

Before we can realize who we really are, we must become conscious of the fact that the person that we think we are, here and now, is at best an imposter and stranger.

—Thomas Merton

Leadership is an elusive calling. That is the beauty of it, really. It is not simply doing a series of tangible acts or practices. It is not a technocratic endeavor. There is no recipe. As a friend of mine once said about leadership, "You don't always know when it's present, but you sure know when it's missing."

The grand paradox in today's climate is that while leadership cannot always be quantified, leaders are expected to be the great quantifiers. They have to get the numbers; they need to produce the so-called bottom line in absolute measurable terms.

While leader performance is often whittled down to a few numbers, the context of organizations is not so simple. Contemporary organizations are complex, yet we want simple metrics that gauge success using a few grand numbers. Maybe we think it has to be that way, particularly since the challenges we face are difficult.

In response, we try to organize life and get a grip on events through multi-layered fragmentation. The paradox is that we fragment organizations in order to create a sense of control over the whole. We separate people into specialties, and then complain that they do not see the whole picture. We split our organizations, interactions, relationships, knowledge, and even people into categories, departments, and interests. We analyze situations and break problems into component parts, and then try to solve them by fine-tuning these parts, as if curing the part heals the whole. We lose the integral character of nature and organizations—their inclusively and unity.

The critical questions are: Is leadership simply a study in deductive reasoning and its application? Why can some leaders mobilize people, develop great commitment, and garner people's loyalty, when others cannot? If leading were pure "science," wouldn't we find the formula and be able to replicate commitment and performance time and again in different environments? Is leadership simply a series of techniques applied with logical and strategic precision? Or does it owe more to the internal life of the leader than to external methods and tactics? Is it just a matter of science, or is there an intangible aspect of leaders that speaks to their journey through life, the wisdom they acquire, and their intention in leading?

LEADERSHIP: WHAT IS THE RISK?

In almost every conversation about leadership, someone will say that leaders are risk takers. That is true. Generally, the risk is seen as proposing programs, making recommendations, or setting a direction. Leaders certainly do these things, and they must be done. But are they really all that risky? Or is the peril more personal than that?

A significant difference exists between one's job and one's work. Making proposals and recommendations is part of the leader's job. While controversy may center on how a leader approaches "the job," the real risk may be in doing our work and making ourselves and our passion known.

Our work, or calling in life, is who we are, why we are here, and how we contribute our talents to the greater world. Our work is how we add our voice to the world. Doing our work is more than completing the tasks or responsibilities in a role description. There is something deeper within each of us that calls us to serve. Our work, while difficult and at times confusing, is not drudgery if it is our calling. Our work has a missionary zeal to it, and as we get lost in it time passes with enormous speed because we are focused and in a state of flow. We do not work to live; but we live to work and meet our calling. A job is too small for us to live. A calling is the principled and moral aspect of a leader's work and obligation.

The poet Mary Oliver, in "The Journey," writes:

> One day you finally knew
> what you had to do, and began,
> though the voices around you
> kept shouting
> their bad advice—[1]

The biggest risk for each of us is finding what it is we have to do with our lives. For some, it is leading school districts, for others it is painting landscapes, and for others it is patrolling neighborhoods in a police cruiser. The voices Oliver speaks of may be our parents, our friends, our spouses, or our own self-imposed limitations and doubts that stop us from pursuing the work we were made to do. Sometimes those voices speak to us out of concern for our welfare, and other times those voices may be self-serving.

Those voices frequently call us back to what others expect of us or to the safety of what we think is practical, respectable, or proper. Some people pursue careers to meet the wishes of their parents or others. Many subsequently give up their college training as teachers or lawyers, give up their positions, and pursue the work and passion they *must* follow—that they are called to do by their inner voice. Following one's bliss is not fanciful or superficial; it is at the core of the purpose of life's journey and happiness. There are, however, no guarantees of success, external recognition, or material gain.

Oliver goes on:

> . . . But little by little,
> as you left their voices behind,
> the stars began to burn
> through the sheets of clouds,
> and there was a new voice
> which you slowly
> recognized as your own,
> that kept you company
> as you strode deeper and deeper
> into the world,
> determined to do
> the only thing you could do—
> determined to save
> the only life you could save.

The voice Oliver hears comes from inside and speaks with an intuitive flare and does not always rely on logic in its messages. This voice echoes from deep in our subconscious and our souls, gnawing at us whenever it is ignored, and becoming the voice of longing when we turn a deaf ear to it.

The kind of leader we are can be victimized by those external voices urging us to behave in particular ways and approach obligations in a prescribed manner. External voices may drown out our inner voice and our individuality and character. The call is to stay in the mold and "on track." Myths and doing business as usual do not always mesh with pursuing a calling with integrity.

Finding our own voice in our work is not just an issue for writers or artists as they develop their craft to find the best way to express themselves. It is also an issue for leaders. Behaving in ways alien to principles, sense of duty, or true self and persona is playing a role, not following our passion or bliss. Role-playing is fine for actors in a stage play, but it is disaster for leaders, because leading is not a role to be played. It has to do with authentic, mature, and honest relationships that continually emerge and evolve.

Playing roles is like painting by the numbers: we institute processes or pursue ventures because of conventional wisdom or because other leaders—our peer group—expect us to act in prescribed ways. The tyranny of the peer group works in the professions as it does in the social world of adolescents. For example, a lawyer who approaches the law in a nonconfrontational and nonadversarial manner may be perceived as too naive and outside the norm by his more adversarial colleagues. Breaking the mold and being willing to stand alone, in harmony with your calling, is a big risk.

The drive in the professions for conformity is immense. Practice must be professional, but that does not mean that professionals have to be plastic people who hide behind unemotional and expressionless masks—all following similar routines. People enter their profession because of passion and a sense of dedication and service to people. While there are ethical and accepted practices, professions are not simply about applying technical treatment and using exclusive jargon. If following a technical manual was all there was to teaching, law, medicine, or leadership, then anyone who read the manual could practice them. Leaders need to find their own voice, their own gait, and apply their knowledge and skills in ways that have integrity with regard to who they are as individuals and the standards and ethics of the profession. True professionals know when to take the lead and deviate from accepted practice in an ethically appropriate manner.

> We will discover the nature of our particular genius when we stop trying to conform our own to other people's models, learn to be ourselves, and allow our natural channel to open.
>
> —Shakti Gawain

Leaders must behave in ways that have integrity in terms of who they are and need to be as professionals and in terms of the profession itself. Otherwise they are on the road to disillusionment and frustration. Repressing our inner soul and purpose is dangerous to our well-being, and ultimately to our success. Living one's life to please others spells danger and results in a life left unexamined and unfulfilled. A life based on other's expectations is empty of meaning and frequently catches us in the web of status and ego. We can lose who we are and what we really want to do if we just collect titles that give us status but do not fulfill us as people. When we retire, or if the title is removed, we can find ourselves lost and empty. Pursuing our calling does not rest on ego satisfaction or status.

Putting off your calling for tomorrow . . . next year . . . or the future is hazardous to your sense of wholeness. Leaders speak their truth, and that means they speak it to themselves as well. They do not create pretenses or deceive themselves. But the truth is wild. It is dangerous; it upsets things and sometimes chafes and rubs at our ego, conventional wisdom, and accepted practice. Speaking the truth carries risk. Leaders live in a context filled with turmoil but presenting great opportunities. Not speaking out and engaging is contrary to leading.

We should be thankful for those challenges nonetheless. In taking the risk of following what we are called to do, we live life with urgency. The poem "Otherwise," by Jane Kenyon, reminds us of the urgency with which we should live life and risk following our bliss. The last stanza states:

> At noon I lay down
> with my mate. It might
> have been otherwise.
> We ate dinner together
> at a table with silver
> candlesticks. It might
> have been otherwise.
> I slept in a bed
> in a room with paintings
> on the walls, and
> planned another day
> just like this day.
> But one day, I know,
> it will be otherwise.[2]

While Kenyon cautions us to live now because one day it will be otherwise, she also awakens us to enjoying the everyday things of life, the pleasures and relationships we have with people and the natural world. In our work, the fabric of relationships brings joy, even when things are difficult. We should cherish each daily opportunity to serve people and to pursue our life's work, because someday it will be otherwise.

Relationships, professional and personal, are reality for leaders. It will never be otherwise. Technology will not change that, and neither will circumstances. People and the relationships we have with them are all we have in life. Valuing people and those connections requires genuine love and a feeling of delight over the similarities and differences they bring to their work. We must respect other people, for they too are called to a unique destiny and their own path.

For leaders, being genuine and authentic in relationships means getting outside of our roles and dissolving our masks. A big risk for leaders is making ourselves known as real people working in relationship with others.

WHAT IS AUTHENTIC?

Frequently people, particularly leaders, identify themselves with their role. Their significance and self-worth in life become intertwined and melded with their title or position. But we are not our roles. One day we will have to stand on our own, without title, prestige, or perks. What of that day? Who will we see in the mirror that morning?

Playing a role is far different from "being" in a role. We are not our role description; we are "beings" in relationship to ourselves, to others, and to our work. Some leaders are comfortable with themselves only when they are "acting" as superintendent, CEO, lawyer, or politician. They become restless creatures away from work, absorbed in cell phones, laptops, faxes, and e-mail—unable to live in and enjoy the moment, or find peace in silence or solitude.

Demons can chase them, resulting in their becoming addicted to the adrenaline rush of demands, challenges, and conflict. The contradiction is that when they are tied up at work, they yearn for quiet time at home with family, friends, or themselves. Identifying our value solely with our job and title cannot satisfy this yearning and the need to fulfill ourselves and find significance.

The great jazz tenor saxophone player Stan Getz felt those demons. When he was at home, he yearned for the excitement of the road. When he was on the road, he yearned for the solitude of home. He could not find the balance that is necessary for a healthy lifestyle and career. His genius and creativity led him to destructive tendencies in his relationships and with his own health and welfare. He restlessly abandoned the present moment for another time and another place, losing the balance in life. He felt "whole" when playing music and was clothed in restlessness at other times.

Our calling must be balanced with our other relationships and purpose. The yearning to pursue our calling is a battle between our real selves and our ego. Ego attracts us, like moths, to the eye of the flame, to build a reputation, to "make things happen," and to stack up accomplishments for our resumes. It builds and strengthens the facade of our indispensability and invincibility. While the flame of ego burns, the candle is consuming itself, leading to our ultimate mortality. Our sense of self-importance and indispensability belie our ultimate mortality. Ego lives in the First World, and our longing seeks the Second World.

Our egos can cause us to put on our plastic masks, adopt clichéd speech and behavior, and bury our true nature. We become actors in our own lives, as well as on the community stage. We confuse motion with movement and doing with being. Roles and pretenses—putting the best face on matters—and creating the appearance of being in control dominate our lives.

At the same time we yearn to be true to ourselves. Deep inside we know when we are out of our natural character and when we compromise our inherent understanding of who we are. We do not want to be an imposter or stranger, as Merton says at the beginning of this chapter. The journey of knowing ourselves may take us through the cactus patch of ego and the barren First World of status and materialism.

Ultimately we cannot run from our inner spirit and ourselves. James Hillman, the noted psychologist, believes that when we die we leave behind our character. "One's remaining image, the unique way of being and doing, left in the minds of others" is what people remember about us.[3] They don't remember our bank account or resume. He believes that what ultimately shines through the history of our life is our real character and genuine self.

The most difficult risk leaders take is exposing their authentic selves. By being true, we become vulnerable to success and failure. Too many people confuse vulnerability with weakness. Authenticity seems like a vague, esoteric term. But in its fundamentals it is a matter of living in this world as we were intended and honestly facing the bright and shadow sides of ourselves. Being authentic is an act of honesty and dependability because it means being true to our character, talents, and spirit. If we are authentic, people know who we are and that they can depend on us to be reliable and stable—we become trustworthy. Making ourselves known in everything we do and in every relationship is what life is about, and it involves showing our "being" in its truest sense and fullest color.

Bill George, former CEO of Medtronic, the world's leading medical technology company, succinctly summarized the qualities of authentic leaders. Authentic leaders:

- genuinely desire to serve others through leadership;
- want to empower others;
- are guided by compassion and passion;
- build enduring relationships; and
- understand their natural abilities, recognize their shortcomings, and are disciplined.[4]

Authentic leaders understand their purpose, live their principles, lead with heart and head, and model values in their relationships.

Being authentic takes courage and embodies the intangible qualities people seek in leaders. That's the irony. Leaders who exhibit the "soft" quality of vulnerability attract, rather than deflect, people through inner peace and fidelity. There are no "shields" when we are genuine because we put ourselves on the line, are accountable, and deal with people in their face-to-face reality. We address their concerns, anger, and reservations directly and personally without the buffers of bureaucracy or the defensiveness of fear.

Because they walk into the face of adversity, with no insulation from subordinates or others, vulnerable leaders are willing to suffer the painful consequences of people's ire, rejection, and anger. Anyone can be tough from a distance, looking through field glasses at the conflict below or standing behind regulations and impersonal procedures. Seeing people on their own turf and meeting them on human, face-to-face terms take courage and openness to people and their lives.

Authentic leaders are not defensive; they treat people as adults, and, as a consequence, they get "unexpressed," "repressed," or submerged feelings from people that may have been festering for ages. People can harbor long-standing resentment, frustration, and disappointment. Stating "unexpressed feelings" can free energy in positive ways and release a load from people's shoulders, but they are not always easy for a leader to hear.

The masks we wear in our role-playing and the pressures we feel are partly born from the multiple expectations we face as leaders. Leaders live with expectations; some self-imposed and related to who they are and what they want to be, and others forced on them by others and the context in which they toil. These multiple expectations come from peers, parents, community, unions, political figures, agencies, legislators, judges, and a host of others.

The expectations coming from such diverse groups are not consistent or congruent. Trying to meet all of them can cause a person to twist and contort in order to achieve them and win favor. Leaders who dance the jig of multiple expectations can lose themselves and their authenticity. They lose their integrity and sense of efficacy by chasing contrary goals, ultimately losing credibility, which is the coin for leadership. Leaders must be grounded in the clay of their deepest beliefs and principles, because the pressure of expectation can generate behavior alien to one's true nature.

Authenticity is not telegraphing to the world all of our deepest thoughts, desires, and feelings, or casting light on the darkest shadows of our souls. There are things in our minds, hearts, and souls that should stay within us. Our inner world of secret feelings and fantasies about ourselves is not appropriate to share with the universe. It is strictly private. However, we can genuinely expose our feelings, principles, and beliefs about our profession and the events of the world. In doing so, we become vulnerable because people see where our passion resides, and any rejection of our passion hurts.

Authenticity presupposes that we know ourselves. But as our life's journey unfolds, we know this is no simple task. Human beings are complex and are pieces of art in the making, being shaped and honed by events and relationships. We are constantly learning about ourselves, which comes from the insight we gain in relationships with others—our loved ones, colleagues, acquaintances, and adversaries—and even in unexpected and poignant interactions with strangers.

Leaders know their strengths and weaknesses, and learn from their errors. Some of us, however, fear making or exposing mistakes. Spanish poet Antonio Machado has a wonderful perspective on mistakes. He says in the poem "Last Night I Had a Dream,"

> Last night I had a dream—
> a blessed illusion it was—
> I dreamt of a hive at work
> deep down in my heart.
> Within were the golden bees
> straining out the bitter past
> to make sweet-tasting honey,
> and white honeycomb.[5]

Straining out the bitter past—mistakes, failures, shortcomings—and turning it into sweet honey takes courage and insight. The errors we make are not to be hidden, nor are they a mark of incompetence or irresponsibility. The issue is not whether we err—it is what we do with the mistakes we make. Like the bees, we can make these mistakes into the honey of our success. Through reflection we accept our efforts, great or small, and our successes or failures. These mistakes can clarify the nature of success and provide insight into ourselves by holding a mirror in front of us, reflecting our skills, character, relationships, passion, and personality.

Withstanding failure requires that we develop a deep understanding of ourselves, which is the ultimate focus of our life's journey. Straining out our bitter memories tempers us to cope with the pain and sorrow of life. As people, we have our private, internal selves and the public selves we share with others and the world. Leaders need to understand their internal selves in order to meet their calling in the external world. Understanding, however, does not always come from success; failure can be quite a catalyst.

Some aspects of us are crystal clear and visible to others and to us. Other parts of us are hidden from others but clear to us. And at times we may be blind to parts of us that others see clearly. There may also be features of our character unknown to others and to us until some circumstance or person sheds light on those features. Maybe this is why some people seem mysterious and take us by surprise.

Johari's window is a mental model for looking at ourselves and our relationships. It highlights that what we show of ourselves to others depends on our relationships. In many relationships, we as leaders may not reveal much of ourselves and remain closed for fear of being uncovered. In such cases, the area open to others may be quite small, and relationships may be highly formal. In an intimate relationship, however, we let down our pretenses and reveal ourselves with all our foibles and fears, because we feel safe and loved.

We also have blind spots. These spots are sometimes exposed by our formal and informal interactions with others. Someone might say, "Whenever there is confusion and ambiguity in situations, you defer to the loudest voice in the room." We might indeed respond that way and not be conscious of it until someone points it out. Then we can examine the reason within us for responding that way.

Johari's window to our inner selves also has a hidden area where no one can tread but ourselves, even in the most intimate relationships. These are the most personal areas of us—our fantasies, fears, and hurts that we do not let others see. Our hidden self is an area of the window we spend a good share of our life exploring. It is not clear to us, and periodically reflections flash before us, providing insight.

To open this window, we must turn our vision inward. A crisis, for example, can highlight an aspect of the hidden part of us. You know people have experienced "insight" when they say "I never thought I would react that way," or "I didn't think I could ever respond to a situation like that," or "I didn't really know I felt that way until now." Those are times when we learn about ourselves and the window to our hidden self opens wider. Personally, I was not aware—until I experienced such an insight—that I was angry with my father for dying when I was four years old. It seemed unfair because heart attacks take lives without consent. I felt angry because I missed him, felt "different" because I did not have a father, and I wanted to know him and have a relationship with him.

Artists, poets, and other creative people are constantly in search of their own truth as individuals. They risk letting us know them, and they also make the world known to us from their perspective. Art is a risky business in that it is so self-revealing. At times, we are surprised at what comes out of our own pens. Like leadership, art carries with it the risk of rejection, ridicule, and condescension. We must affirm our belonging and stand by our deepest knowledge and identity.

How many of us as leaders leave the attitude that we know everything? With our attachments and our "open" window, many of us feel uncomfortable when we get into situations beyond our knowing in our professional or private lives. The press of expectations and our own ego restrict us to the safety of one room in which the furniture is worn and comfortable, the lighting is perfect, and the smells of familiarity and security fill the air.

Knowing ourselves—uncovering the hidden areas of our character and soul—is a risky business that carries us into uncharted waters. Can leaders lead without being adroit at understanding themselves and having the rootedness to move into the fog of uncertainty and confusion that calls for true leadership?

Finding our voice and who we are does not come only from interaction with others. Many great leaders have had time—in some cases imposed through imprisonment or other circumstances—to go inside and learn about themselves, to make connections between ideas and thoughts, and to develop frames of mind that have helped them adapt to the rigors of leadership. Nelson Mandela, Senator John McCain, President Theodore Roosevelt, Dr. Martin Luther King Jr., the Dalai Lama, Mohandas Gandhi, and so many others had to travel a difficult road to get to the point at which their leadership was right for the times. They had a "vision," to use a term bloated from overuse, and had a sense of peace and perspective that got them through difficult times. Difficulty and tragedy in life can reveal our sense of purpose.

What do we need to become authentic and genuine as leaders? Silence and stillness are two things that are rare in the life of organizations, with all their technology, meetings, immediacy, and panic. Wisdom does not come without reflection.

The pace of life has accelerated, and television, cell phones, faxes, and the suburbanization of the countryside have invaded times and spaces for solitude. At times we are physically present, but we are not available to our families, our friends, or ourselves. We don't live in the moment because we're looking to the past or worrying about the future. And in a real way, we are not available to the people with whom we work because our minds are stuffed full of schedules, deadlines, meetings, priorities, work product, and doing, doing, doing. We have little chance to just "be" at work or away from it because we seldom have the solitude of authentic life. Our minds are clogged—filled—and they run at a frenetic speed.

Ironically, our technology, which helps us complete complex tasks quickly, has not helped us find solitude and peace. Instead, it makes us instantly available, almost everywhere at any time, encroaching on our lives. Taming the dysfunctions technology brings to schools and the workplace is essential if we are to find quiet reflective time and peace. Otherwise each moment is lost, and eventually we lose the balance we require to use our knowledge, intuition, and faculties.

Silence is essential for us to hear the inner voice that wants to tell us what is on its mind and what song it is singing. Becoming known to the world is telling your story and opening your window in an appropriate manner to let people know who you are. Aloofness spells distance, and leaders who are distant from those they lead are doomed to playing roles. One teacher said of her superintendent, who had worked in the district for four years, "I guess he did OK. We didn't see him much. We never really knew who he was as a person."

Not knowing the leader "as a person" produces remoteness and lost opportunities for mutual growth.

Leaders do not have to inappropriately tell their secrets: the hidden part of the window should remain that way. But people do want to hear and know the leaders' stories—what's on their mind, what are their aspirations, what are their disappointments. Stories are very compelling. People want to connect to leaders as much as leaders want to connect to the people they lead. Allowing silence into our organizations and our lives helps us hear one another. Slowing the pace enables us to share our professional passions and helps us understand why we became leaders in the first place.

In seeking new leaders for schools, many people identify passion as a positive characteristic in a superintendent or principal. Great leaders live not only with passion but also with fervor. They welcome challenge. Some day it will be otherwise, so they should take advantage of tackling the big issues of the day. Leaders who want to squirrel away their "political capital" and save it for another day may be disappointed, because that day may never come. Caution can compromise our promise.

Each of us has only a limited time in life to pursue our passion, to meet our calling, to have an impact on the big issues of the day, and to love the ones we hold dear. Kenyon's poem speaks of that and of finding balance in our lives to enjoy the simple pleasures of a perfect day. Someday, it really will be otherwise.

NOTES

1. Oliver, Mary. "The Journey," in *New and Selected Poems*. Boston: Beacon, 1992, pp. 114–15.

2. Kenyon, Jane. "Otherwise," in *Otherwise: New and Selected Poems*. St. Paul: Graywolf Press, 1996, p. 214.

3. Hillman, James. *The Force of Character*. New York: Random House, 1999, p. xxx.

4. George, Bill. *Authentic Leadership*. San Francisco: Jossey-Bass, 2003.

5. Machado, "Last Night I Had a Dream," *Selected Poems*. Cambridge, MA: Harvard University Press, 1982, p. 91.

6

Leadership and the Creative Universe

The most beautiful thing we can experience is the mysterious.

—Albert Einstein

The real art of discovery consists not in finding new lands but in seeing with new eyes.

—Marcel Proust

As you swim in the seas of leadership, you soon realize that there are mysterious things at play. Because of our inclination to want to control things, however, we don't always see the mysterious as beautiful. We lose the attraction of the universe and the opportunities that come with life. These seas are susceptible to unexpected winds, undertows, or gales—the universe is a place of integral dynamism and uncertainty.

Life is a constantly evolving mosaic, filled with joy and sorrow, success and failure, growth and renewal. Poets, philosophers, and physicists seem to understand this pattern of life better than organizational theorists and business leaders.

Mary Oliver, in the poem "Wild Geese," talks of the natural world and our place in it.

> You do not have to be good.
> You do not have to walk on your knees
> for a hundred miles through the desert, repenting.
> You only have to let the soft animal of your body
> love what it loves.
> Tell me about despair, yours, and I will tell you mine.
> Meanwhile the world goes on.

Meanwhile the sun and the clear pebbles of the rain
are moving across the landscapes,
over the prairies and the deep trees,
the mountains and the rivers.
Meanwhile the wild geese, high in the clean blue air,
are heading home again.
Whoever you are, no matter how lonely,
the world offers itself to your imagination,
calls to you like the wild geese, harsh and exciting—
over and over announcing your place
in the family of things.[1]

Oliver's poem has many lessons for leaders. She speaks of allowing ourselves to do what comes naturally as we live in this world and become a part of it—authentically and genuinely, with all our frailties and all our humanness in facing the challenges and inevitable pain of life. We should reach for the imagination the world offers and respond in our own creative way to the exciting and harsh realities facing us. When we fall short, we don't have to repent. Leaders must be in harmony with the world and accept it as it is, with its rhythms and cycles, and not torment ourselves when things go awry or try to manage the unmanageable. We can only do the best we can.

Oliver does not see people as living divorced from world—separate and alone. Leadership mythology presents leaders as plagued by separation and loneliness. Oliver uses the word "family" to indicate our interconnected relationship with one another and the natural world—ties that cannot be broken by political, cultural, economic, or social structures. She declares our integral and interconnected nature in the following lines:

the world offers itself to your imagination,
calls to you like the wild geese, harsh and exciting—
over and over announcing your place
in the family of things.

Not controlling the universe does not relegate us to the role of victim. As leaders we are able to respond to the world around us, including unexpected events and things beyond our control. We can respond because we are not "mistakes among other mistakes," as poet David Whyte notes.[2] We are connected to others and to the universe and have an active place in this beautiful montage called life.

Einstein used the beauty of the mysterious as a beacon to the wonder in all of us. Finding our place allows us to live in the wonder of nature and our own spirit and uniqueness. The world is an imaginative place and we are creative beings who can add to its texture and genius. We can respond through our commitment, creativity, and imagination when opportunities are presented to us. Leadership is about addressing our world and its challenges in an original way using our talents and gifts.

TRUTH AND VISION

A common thread of obligation binds poets and leaders. Both must tell the truth and shed light on the world from a new perspective. Poets share a perspective on life, and leaders must share a vision of the future. Leaders who can paint an inspired picture of the future support people in making a commitment to something larger than their self-interest. They help make sense out of a world that is often electrifying and energizing, as well difficult and confusing.

Forming a personal vision can promote change and open the opportunity for seeing things optimistically and freshly. While creating something new is part of the generative process, so is re-creating ourselves—particularly restoring ourselves to a sense of wholeness. Discovering meaning in our lives as leaders is a generative process requiring us to learn and increase our capacity for understanding and accepting the world, others, and ourselves. Generative learning and creativity are essential for developing insight and wisdom.

Many times we observe but don't really see. In a sense we sleepwalk—with our eyes closed to what surrounds us. Being awake to the potential around us, without the filters of expectation and bias, is essential for leaders to see their own truth. An artist who carves and paints replicas of birds said to me, "I see the world differently. I see birds all over the place. People don't see them; they don't notice what's around them." The problem is that as leaders we don't see the birds, the dynamic world around us; and sometimes we can miss the truth. We can miss the truth of the moment because our vision is blurry, distracted, or limited.

> Let us not look back in anger or in fear but in awareness.
>
> —James Thurber

Vision is an important word in any discussion of leadership. The question is: What kind of vision should a leader have? How do we as leaders see? Is what we see important? One common interpretation is that *vision* refers to an image, an idea, or an aspiration that forms the basis for leadership and program development. Theorists and strategists suggest that leaders build a "shared vision" and future goals for the success of the organization. Our vision, however, can become tired and fuzzy, caught in the web of the clichéd and conventional, nothing more than a used photograph of someone else's life or a carbon copy of what is past.

Life changes each moment. The world is too dynamic for sleepwalking through it. Some ideas do not bear fruit simply because people can't imagine them working at the time. We have to wait for another occasion, when the picture changes and people see things differently.

Chogyam Trungpa is emphatic: "Look. This is your world! You can't not look. There is no other world. This is your world; it is your feast. You inherited this; you inherited these eyeballs; you inherited this world of color. Look at the greatness of the whole thing. Look! Don't hesitate—look! Open your eyes. Don't blink, and look, look—look further."[3]

Leaders, poets, and artists see the world as innocents. They have a childlike view and optimism that keep surprise, optimism, and possibility alive. Statistics, standards, procedures, protocol, and ego do not cloud their vision. Wisdom in life comes, in part, from seeing the wonder of people and things on this planet. Without wonder, originality, imagination, and innovation are silenced, and curiosity and questioning are blanketed. Seeing things again for the first time is a gift and an essential component of leadership.

What kind of vision should leaders have? Hindsight? Foresight? Insight? Should leaders be farsighted or nearsighted? Do they need peripheral or tunnel vision? Vision is much more than simply tossing out a slogan or following empty platitudes. If it does not capture imagination or create energy, it is not vision. It is simply a pedantic slogan.

Actually, leaders need all kinds of vision. To bring a dream or a concept into reality, leaders need to see in many different ways, using a variety of visions:

- *Insight*: For centuries, philosophers have advised leaders, "Know thyself." Insight into ourselves is a critical part of knowing ourselves, our motivation, and our values. Insight is needed for authenticity and genuineness in leadership style, and it also presumes deep understandings of personal values, beliefs, principles, and attachments. A strong sense of self comes only from looking inside and reflecting so we can look ahead.
- *Foresight*: In building a visionary plan, foresight is essential. Having an idea of what is about to emerge, not simply what is already manifest and obvious to everyone, is a mark of a leader. Seeing around the bend in the road is essential to success, and it often requires a sensitive hand and intuitive abilities. Leaders with foresight have the capacity to understand what is profound and what is temporary and ephemeral. Identifying and understanding driving forces and their impact is a critical factor in knowing the difference between symptoms and causes.

- *Hindsight*: Whoever gave hindsight a bad name did a disservice. Sure, hindsight is 20/20, but analyzing and replaying past events also creates "future memory" so the same mistakes are not made in similar circumstances in the future. Hindsight also sheds light on areas that were ignored and identifies the dynamics that touched people's hearts and minds positively or negatively. Hindsight pinpoints how events unfolded and highlights the intangibles that shaped past events, frequently reminding us of the limitations of data and the power of intangibles. Continued growth can come from hindsight, and learning sprouts from both success and failure. The key is to not obsess about past issues and become frozen in the past.
- *Farsight and Nearsight*: Looking down the road requires a keen eye to anticipate issues. Farsightedness allows us to play out the consequences of current decisions and initiatives, as well as observe the influence of the driving forces at play. Farsight assists us with foreseeing issues and capturing the initiative of future events. However, being nearsighted can help us see the local impact close to home. Acting locally has a big impact globally. Global thinking and local action are essential to clarifying what is emerging and defining how it affects people at home. Local preparation and anticipation require both near- and farsight.
- *Peripheral and Tunnel Vision*: Leaders need a wide-angle lens to see the entire shape and integral tone of the landscape in which they work. This conceptual lens offers a broad perspective, allowing leaders to see dynamics and interconnections. Every now and then, we need to get out of our tunnels and use our peripheral vision to see what is happening in other sectors or contexts that may affect us. We also need a strong focus on important issues and initiatives that affect our organizations and context. If we focus on minor issues, a great dysfunction can occur: major issues become minor, and minor ones become major, skewing talent and sapping resources. Tunnel vision and sharp, concentrated focus can create the energy and intensity needed to get specific initiatives completed, initiatives that take advantage of larger dynamics or can quell or compromise the negative effects of them.

Being a "visionary" leader means being an "integral leader"[4]—one who brings together people and sees in an inclusive, balanced, and comprehensive way, embracing science, nature, art, ethics, the disciplines, and the sociopolitical-economic context. Such leaders look in places outside their fields for ideas, trends, driving forces, and associations.

Getting a new perspective outside our own profession can highlight innovative approaches and directions. Leaders need to be awake to the dynamics, both delicate and obvious, that affect local and national educational issues. As Chogyam Trungpa suggests, we need to take time to see and not be blinded by blizzards of paper or the fog of emotion or bias. We must keep our eyes on our intentions and be able to ask the right questions to move them toward their realization.

Artists have visions. They express ideas about the world and reflect the positive and negative aspects of humanity. A leader's values and experience also produce a perspective for seeing the world, events, and people, in both positive and negative lights. A leader's perspective can appeal to the best in us or fan the fears within us. Some leaders' visions are immoral and dark. Hitler, Stalin, and Pol Pot were bad seeds who appealed to the dark side and evil purposes to tyrannize people. Visions can be pedantic or noble. They can motivate people through the spectrum to positive light or pull them to darkness. Visions and intentions can shed light on new ideas and new ways.

LEADERSHIP AND CREATIVITY

Creativity has as much to do with our spiritual side as leaders as it does with our cognitive perception and thinking. Leadership is not simply planning, making decisions, and strategizing.

Creative leadership has to do with giving, which has to do with our calling because as leaders we are "beckoned" to share our talents and abilities and to contribute without expecting anything in return. Leadership is an act of altruism.

Leadership is an act of the human spirit. Following one's calling to make the world for children better is indeed a spiritual and loving act. In stewardship, leaders give by leaving a gift of their talent and their contributions. Creativity and calling are aspects of love, and to love is to share our gifts with the world and others. In addition, leaders help others share their talents and authentic selves to contribute to the common good. By doing so, leaders show respect and affection for humanity and the people with whom we work.

The theologian Meister Eckhart believes that to be creative is to be in touch with and be willing to express our inner person. He says: "Whatever can be truly expressed in its proper meaning must emerge from inside a person and pass through the inner form. It cannot come from outside to inside of a person, but must emerge from within."[5]

Creativity has its source in our deepest roots and essence as human beings. When we act creatively, we experience "the ecstasy of enchantment" and see the world anew. Creativity is not simply caused by lightening-bolt inspiration that unexpectedly strikes out of the dark. Applying our gifts is an act of the human will and spirit, involving a commitment to disciplined practice and an understanding of classic approaches.

Eckhart also sees creativity as a means of healing. A creative act, whether in art or leadership, heals the distance between our inner and outer selves. It is an act of salvation in that we see, through a creative experience, our common humanity and talents. Creativity sheds light on our truth—who we are—as a means to give back to others.

According to Eckhart, one of the definitive creative states of beauty and grace is compassion, because rebirth occurs in a spirit of selflessness. Compassion and understanding heal and create a sense of belonging: they are not signs of weakness. People can re-create themselves in a caring environment, and creative leaders can re-create themselves and help others fulfill their destiny—both of which are no small achievements.

> The man with new ideas is a crank until the idea succeeds.
>
> —Mark Twain

Creativity, as a generative process, requires mindfulness. The greatest learning occurs because of what we notice; and what we notice is, in part, a result of our experience and relationships, which can alter our perspective and shed more light on who we are both inside ourselves and in the outer world. In human terms, learning forces us to re-create ourselves, to think about our lives anew, to ask whether we live with integrity, and to do the work we were meant to do. Insights can lead to new behavior and purpose.

Re-creation is a thorny and unsettling process that spurs creativity because it causes us to view conditions and ourselves in a different light and from a different angle. The stakes are high, particularly for leaders, because there is the prospect of failure and loss.

Creative leaders tackle two risks: the risk of re-creation—going inside themselves and confronting how they live their lives—and the risk of giving up the comfort of the known and embracing ambiguity and growth. In both cases, the attachment to security, self-image, and external expectations is at risk. An external risk for creative people is to be considered out of the mainstream or even bizarre. Truly creative people who "march to a different drummer" often present innovative ideas that are scoffed at initially and then accepted. The proponents of CNN, flight, FedEx, talking films, and the personal computer were all scoffed at by people.

Creativity is a challenging urge because it may involve disappointment and possibly rejection. Shakespeare, in *As You Like It*, touches on this risk:

> Sweet are the uses of adversity,
> Which the toad, ugly and venomous
> Wears yet a precious jewel in his head;
> And this our life, exempt from public haunt,
> Finds tongues in trees, books in running brooks,
> Sermons in stone, and good in everything.[6]

When we curse the darkness and adversity, sweetness, in the form of new opportunities and learning, may help imaginative solutions blossom. Adversity helps us uncover and observe subtle nuances, and may change our minds and perspectives. Growth is seldom a painless and risk-free process, because it is difficult to give up our ways of thinking and our mindset.

The risks are also greater if we are involved with issues about which we feel passion and love, both driving forces of creativity. In this situation the ante is greater because the potential for personal loss and pain is greater. Taking an untried course with something we love is dicey—the stakes are high and our fears aroused. Without emotion, creativity, and passion, leadership becomes devoid of vigor, and the organization cannot be awakened to operate with greater levels of integrity and wholeness.

Burning passion, perseverance, and creativity are all linked intimately. Learning how to fail better in the course of finding new solutions is a creative venture that takes the virtue of perseverance and the risk of failure. Perseverance and action, when we are confronted with the logic of data that dictate a different course, take courage and freedom from the chains of predictable practice.

Freedom is one of our great longings—freedom to be who we must be, freedom to pursue our purpose, freedom to connect with the world in our own significant way, and freedom to create and to apply our talents and our heartfelt energy. The freedom to be oneself, however, is not restricted to leaders.

Leaders must develop the climate for nurturing creativity in others by establishing the crucible—the setting—in which others are free to contribute their talents and reach for a higher purpose. Rigid control restricts imagination and breeds conformity and closed perspectives. Freedom is essential because it challenges conviction, builds enthusiasm, and forms order around values and principles. Freedom to make mistakes with integrity is a mark of a generative organization, because missteps enlighten focus, raise new questions, and uncover new ways.

Freedom and creativity produce a sense of wholeness and efficacy. Motivation is easy when people are free to follow their passion and contribute to something significant. All living systems, including organizations, generate, learn, and evolve or they die. Staid and stale organizations face their demise unless they are resourceful and adaptive to survive and thrive in circumstances unfolding down the road.

Creativity requires a conversation about ideals and principles. The process of dialogue unifies people so that in their individual and collective freedom they can move forward with greater understanding of all issues and positions, as well as a respect for different visions. Emergence of new ideas is the offspring of conversation and creativity.

In creative learning environments ideas, processes, possibilities, conflicts, innovations, and new structures emerge in response to the trials and issues facing us. Ideas should not come only from the leader. Ideas surface from all corners because leadership is distributed and interaction is constant. People self-organize through dialogue. In an ant colony, which is actually a fairly good model for complex organizations, there is no super ant leading the way and directing traffic. The ants in the colony communicate using only nine to twenty different communication "signals," and they self-organize in order to have ample food, clear the tunnels of debris, and provide safety and order. Without one leader to give orders the ants self-organize because of ongoing and consistent "local" communication between individual ants. There is not an "engineering department," CEO, or board of directors—just individual ants living in community, connected individually to each other and communicating clear, simple messages. As a result, the ants construct complex and thriving colonies—all without a hierarchical leader.

Self-organizing systems respond continuously to change, which is an organizing, not a dysfunctional, force. Margaret Wheatley states, "Structure and solutions are temporary. . . . Leaders emerge from the needs of the moment. There are far fewer levels of management. Experimentation is the norm."[7]

She specifies the three conditions for self-organizing systems: identity, information, and relationships. Identity is an intent and who we think we are as a group. Information is what we choose to notice through our lens of identity. Information "lies at the heart of life"[8] that helps us organize "in-formation." It has to be everywhere and shared in self-organizing systems. The more access people have to one another, the greater the possibilities and the sharing of insight.

Leaders help nurture and ensure distributed leadership across the "network" of relationships. In such an environment, people can self-organize and use their talents and imagination toward common goals and values. Creative organizations with a sense of wholeness have a tight focus and dynamic, as well as consistent dialogue.

David Whyte's poem "What I Must Tell Myself" has a stanza that highlights the generative process and interconnectivity:

> When one thing dies all things
> die together, and must live again
> in a different way,
> when one thing
> is missing everything is missing,
> and must be found again
> in a new whole
> and everything wants to be complete,
> everything wants to go home
> and the geese traveling south

are like the shadow of my breath
flying into the darkness
on great heart-beats
to an unknown land where I belong.[9]

This stanza speaks of creativity, regeneration and renewal, and integral wholeness in good or difficult times. Our interconnected values and our personal nature help us to face the joy and pain of life, and celebrate the life cycles of growth and regeneration. Whyte sees in this cycle of regeneration the longing to belong and a yearning for wholeness and connection. Despite being categorized into roles and areas of specialization in our organizational life, we yearn for a sense of efficacy—that sense of interconnection and place in the order of things that give us completeness.

Creativity and wholeness are essential in the complex web of social and professional relationships. Leaders, however, fear having the organization plunge into discord and dysfunction, and they have great concern about losing control, because, according to conventional wisdom, leaders are to "take care of things." They get terrified by the vagueness, insecurity, and ambiguity of what might happen in a creative and emergent environment in which people self-organize and external controls are not present.

Gil Evans, the noted jazz arranger and bandleader, was famous for his creativity and new approaches. He gave his musicians freedom to improvise and follow their imaginative impulses. In fact, soloists and the entire ensemble would improvise around his sketchy musical charts. He states in a *Downbeat Magazine* interview:

> We don't even need written music anymore. Hiriam [Bullock] or I strike a chord and away we will go, improvising ensembles and everything for 10 or 15 minutes. I tell the players not to be terrified by the vagueness.
>
> If it looks like we're teetering on the edge of formlessness, somebody's going to be panicked and they'll do something about it. I depend on that. If it has to be me, I'll do it, but I'll wait and wait because I want somebody else to do it. I want to hear what's going to happen.[10]

Evans' orchestra was an example of a self-organizing and generative group. It was individually and collectively creative, as soloists stretched their improvisation and the rest of the ensemble improvised in return. Confronting the ambiguity of creativity takes nerve because it is not convenient—it cannot always be programmed and cannot be manufactured: true performances are risky because the results are not always sure. Leadership, however, is based on creativity, and creativity takes courage and faith. The risk is living on the edge of creativity.

LEADERSHIP AND HEALING

Conflict is inherent in nature. It is also inherent in social systems like organizations and communities. Disagreement and change exist, and leaders are frequently at the center of a conflict between values—the conflict between what is and what can be or the conflict between ego and purpose. There are many kinds of conflict that leaders experience, and in some cases, leaders must have the courage to create conflict.

Conflict can beget turmoil and hurt. More and more frequently, school boards claim that they want a superintendent who can "heal" the district. Thomas Moore said that we too often try to find healing in physicians' and therapists' offices, in answers others give us, or in magic pills. Renewal and healing, however, begin within each of us: facing ourselves and jettisoning anger, searching for balance, and obtaining peace. People who are not at peace cannot create an environment in which others can seek the healing peace that is essential to all of us.

Rachel Carson says, "There is something healing in the repeated refrains of nature—the assurance that dawn comes after the night and spring after winter."[11] Leaders can take solace in that cycle, as well as communicate it to others. The turmoil of life can cause people to think only of the darkness, rather than understand that disequilibrium can produce the light of ideas, energy, and peace. Chaos has limits and boundaries, but with chaotic energy comes creativity and enlightenment.

The conflict and havoc that often engulf leaders can take their toll. Healing—of emotions, feelings, relationships, and connections—may be necessary to prevent the social system from dithering in dysfunction. Certainly when tragedies occur, people need to heal from the trauma of it all.

Healing in organizations is not related solely to crises; it is necessary in the normal course of people working together. Some people feel that others do not listen, others feel impotent, some are hurt when their ideas are rejected, and others feel frustrated when their efforts are not successful. Whenever people work together there are times when healing within and between people is needed. Otherwise, these pains can lead to ineffectiveness and misunderstanding.

To create a healing environment, leaders must realize that they cannot heal others. They do not have that omnipotent power or control. However, they can create the conditions, the context, the vessel, the environment for healing to take place. Leaders can help fashion the climate and culture so that old wounds heal and a positive and healthy environment is created. The organization develops a sense of community and unity; people care about one another.

Organizational healing, very simply, is a return to wholeness: bringing an organization or person back to its full functioning and integrity to meet its purpose. It has to do with harmony between practice and values. Healing relationships are honest and authentic, with no false masks or pretenses. In this context, individuals with distinct views and personalities work toward a common purpose.

Healing is not a cognitive process because we cannot always rationalize events or discover the logic of why things happened as they did. Tragedies happen, work teams struggle, and resources are slight. Feelings and emotions are involved and must be addressed. In healing situations, anger and frustration and a sense of impotence are often intertwined with the pain of loss of self-concept, opportunity, or relationships. Healing is not a slogan on a greeting card: it is much deeper than that and requires leadership to help bring it about.

Healing does not take place in patchwork fashion, nor through the quick fix of a magic pill. As with personal situations, people need time to process their experience and confront situations honestly. Honesty means dealing with conditions and confronting emotions, sometimes very uncomfortable ones. There are no shortcuts on some issues. Time and courage are necessary. Leaders can provide time. But for individuals to have the courage to express feelings in a nondestructive way, to clear the air, and to eliminate negative energy requires safety, the right environment, and the right modeling of the leader.

To create the conditions for healing, first, leaders must understand that healing requires patience, isn't always easy, and takes time. Leaders can help craft the conditions and environment by doing the following:

- Be authentic in your role as a leader—be comfortable with yourself and don't play a role; there are no pretenses or facades. Role-playing is for the movies, not organizations. Being who you are is genuine and conveys a sense of personal wholeness and approachability.
- Speak from the heart—express feeling sincerely. They are powerful, and stating how you feel can help others express their feelings. One way is to speak from the heart and give "I" messages in which feelings are stated clearly and in a nonthreatening manner. For example, "I get anxious when . . ." or "I am unsure how to. . . ." These "I" messages may communicate the very feeling others are experiencing, validating that they feel the same way, and letting them know that they are not alone and that it is safe to express feelings. In the workplace, feelings are often avoided. Nothing is more dysfunctional than ignoring feelings, because it separates people and can create a negative "field" that builds invisible, but deeply felt, barriers. A community of shared feeling, however, can unite people and build understanding.
- Active listening is directly related to "I" messages, but on the other side of the table. In active listening you clarify the content and intent of messages

in a nonjudgmental manner. Simply saying "I hear you say that you are frustrated with . . ." or "I sense that you are angry about . . ." and listening to the response can make a big difference in promoting understanding and letting the person know you are interested and comprehend his or her full meaning.
- People want to be heard and understood—both the content and intent of their messages. Frequently the content (the information being communicated) is not congruent with the intent (the feelings and emotions being relayed). We all have had experiences in which a person communicates a seemingly benign message but the intent and tone of it is anger. The feelings overwhelm the content, or at least cloud it, causing ambiguity or incongruence. Patience is required because people may be reticent about sharing their feelings openly.
- The virtue of active listening is clear. When people feel heard, even if nothing can be done, they feel better. Many times leaders don't have to solve problems, they just have to listen and understand them.

Communicating clearly and honestly and being true to organizational values is essential. Personal integrity is critical if organizational integrity is to be restored. Leaders must behave in accord with principles because doing so reassures people and provides structure and stability.

Leaders who create a climate for healing do not cut along the scars of the past or pick the scabs on old wounds. They look forward and not backward, allowing people to move on anew and not brandish old hurts.

Words are easy . . . true commitment is not. Leaders do not cut and run when things get tough. Building solid relationships requires "hanging in there" and working through the peaks as well as the valleys. Compassion is easy when things are flying high. When dark trouble appears, leadership, compassion, and empathy take courage and are the glue that holds people together in a sense of community and binds wounds.

Leaders submerge ego and act out of stewardship—doing what is best for the long term and leaving the organization in better shape than before, even if they do not get credit or enhance their careers. Stewardship means bringing the organization to a higher state of wholeness and integrity.

Finally, leaders as healers act with compassion, understanding, and forgiveness toward staff, the community, and themselves. Everyone needs compassion and empathy. Quality relationships are based on these qualities, and without them healing cannot take place. When people are battered or bruised by life, they need an environment in which they can be introspective, find silence and peace, and then move on, let things unfold, and build a better future. People seek a sense of community, of belonging, particularly at a time when technology depersonalizes and other dynamics fragment.

NOTES

1. Oliver, Mary. "Wild Geese," in *Owls and Other Fantasies*. Boston: Beacon Press, 2003, p. 1.

2. Whyte, David. *House of Belonging*. Langley, WA: Many Rivers Press, 2002, p. 27.

3. Trungpa, Chogyam. www.zaadz.com.

4. Wilber, Ken. *A Theory of Everything: An Integral Vision for Business, Politics, Science, and Spirituality*. Boston: Shambhala Publications, 2000, p. xii.

5. Fox, Matthew. *Passion for Creation: The Earth-Honoring Spirituality of Meister Eckhart*. Rochester, VT: Inner Traditions, 2000.

6. Shakespeare, William. *As You Like It*. New York: Washington Square Press, 1997, act 2, scene 1.

7. Wheatley, Margaret, and Kellner-Rogers, Myron. *The Irresistible Future of Organizing*. Berkana Institute, www.berkana.org, July/August, 1996.

8. Wheatley, Margaret. *Leadership and the New Science*. San Francisco: Berrett-Koehler, 1992, p. 100.

9. Whyte, David. "What I Must Tell Myself," in *House of Belonging*. Langley, WA: Many Rivers, 2002, p. 14.

10. Evans, Gil. "The Lone Arranger," interview by Mike Zwerin. *Downbeat Magazine*, April 1998.

11. Crider, Tom. *A Nature Lover's Book of Quotations*. Southbury, CT: Birch Tree, 2000, p. 100.

7

Plans, Stories, and Improvisation

The plans you make are too small for you to live.

—David Whyte

Today, everyone is planning. Leaders are planning the next steps in their career, their lives, and their schools. Planning is perceived as essential to a successful and happy life. Letting things unfold is not a notion that is widely accepted, particularly in organizations. Leaders are supposed to focus on strategies to gain control and to move events forward. Certainly, professionals need to plan: the public expects it, and plans can focus effort. Life, however, does not always play out according to our designs and templates, which raises the question of what can be done in addition to traditional planning in order to lead.

The process of planning has added a whole vocabulary to our language—a jargon both technocratic and impersonal. The language speaks of desired outcomes and strategic initiatives seemingly devoid of people, who are dehumanized into stakeholders, constituents, or customers. Real people seem removed from the events or they are viewed as objects or targets of tactics and systems. Numbers become more important than people, as the process reeks of bottom lines, benchmarks, targets, or metrics.

The assumption is that if we make plans, the world and the universe will respond as desired, and that truth is found in collecting and seeing the numbers. "Did we reach our target?" and "How are we doing on the major indicators?" are key questions. Numbers, not people, seem to be the focus. Individual people get lost in averages, medians, and percentages.

All managers try to consider all the "variables." But people are not variables, and the presumption of their control is contrary to how individuals work together. Plans based on linear, cause-and-effect logic wilt in the face of dynamic, self-renewing systems and people's spirit.

While we try to force events and master circumstances that swirl around them, we cannot control time or when and how things emerge. In the natural order of things sometimes the only thing we can do is react. When storms lash the countryside, we can only close the shutters. Sometimes our instruments and strategies are impotent in the face of fields and forces that exist in nature and in people's hearts and souls. We must settle for influence and timing for dynamics to be ready for change.

Our instruments, technology, and computers still cannot forecast our organizational and social weather with certainty, and they certainly cannot foretell how people will relate and interact in the complex web of workplace relationships. Our machines and technology are immune to the fields, forces, and energy of human beings and the heart, imagination and beliefs they bring with them. Controlling people is beyond our scope. The certainty of control is lost in the confluence of people's lives and relationships.

A leader's greatest asset is not the process of planning and analysis but conceptualizing and the application of imagination and creativity. Living in the moment and being able to discern the dynamic forces at work are keys to successful leadership. Knowing when to move and when to stop, when to act and when to be still, when to be silent and when to talk are all intangibles that leaders need to understand. Breaking from or staying with a plan is also a significant decision for a leader to make.

BEYOND WINGING IT: LEADERSHIP AND IMPROVISATION

When school boards define the qualities they desire in a new leader, inevitably they want someone adept at planning. "We want a leader who can implement our strategic plan and get quantifiable results." Few, if any, mention, "We want a person who is an excellent improviser."

As the old saying goes, "The best laid plans . . ." often get derailed in the nonlinear world in which we live. Plans sputter and flop. In this type of world improvising is a great asset. However, improvisation and leadership seem to be strange bedfellows. In a sense, improvisation is the Rodney Dangerfield of leadership—it gets no respect.

Rigidly sticking to plans in a dynamic environment is a recipe for failure. Emotional, nonlinear, nonquantifiable, and hidden forces derail the best of them. What is manifest is not the problem. What is emerging, what is around the bend in the road, is what produces havoc for plans. Chaos and nonrationality prevail and are a part of all open social systems.

Leaders, however, must get the job done—disequilibrium and chaos be damned! Successful leaders know when to stick to a plan and when to improvise. After all, leadership is a creative force building imaginative relationships and networks that respond to situations and issues in a nimble way. How do improvisation and leadership fit together? What are the advantages and hazards of improvisation?

WHY IMPROVISE?

Western scientific method and part-to-whole, cause-and-effect thinking reign in organizations. Based on these assumptions, strategic plans should work and people should act with rational precision. The "machinery" of management should succeed because everyone should do their "part" and respond as anticipated. The spate of leadership books is testament to the error of these notions—if they were foolproof, leaders would only have to implement and monitor plans and they would succeed.

Billy Collins, poet laureate of the United States, in his poem "Butterfly Effect," highlights how the world succumbs to events that seem insignificant and far away, yet have a great impact.

> The one [butterfly] resting now on a plant stem
> somewhere deep in the vine-hung
> interior of South America
> whose wings are about to flutter
> thus causing it to rain heavily
> on your wedding day
> several years from now,
> and spinning you down
> a path to calamity and ruin
> is—if it's any consolation—
> a gorgeous swallowtail,
> a brilliant mix of bright orange
> and vivid yellow with a soft
> dusting of light brown along the edges.[1]

Collins's poem highlights a concept alien to how we normally think in today's organizations. He identifies the small, insignificant, and unnoticed flap of a swallowtail's wings that will have unanticipated and major consequences. While we are taught from our old science books that for every action there is an equal reaction, physicists have discovered the butterfly effect. Action and reaction are not always proportionate. We see it at work when seemingly small things derail a major initiative or minute or random acts are the keys to success.

Butterflies are alive and well in organizations, resting in the interior mindscapes of people, flying the gentle breezes of people's hearts, or fluttering in their fears, passions, and emotions. On the international scene a relatively obscure event can effect a diplomatic nightmare or helpful breakthrough. The butterflies in our lives add serendipity and the need to be flexible and know when to improvise. Butterflies add color and opportunity to our lives in a world full of unseen, immeasurable fields and forces that affect people and plans.

Goals are achieved because of the great insight of leaders to read situations and respond tactically in effective and constructive ways. Leaders face two types of decisions. Substantive decisions concern destinations: the desired goals and objectives—the "whys" and "whats" of plans. On the other hand, tactical or strategic decisions involve the processes and approaches to get to the destination—the "hows" leaders employ to achieve the "whys" and "whats." There is a critical danger with strategic decisions. Successful tactics can be applied to wrong-headed or negative goals. Consequently, the thoughts and values behind substantive decisions are critical to ensure "rightness" and ethical conduct.

Many strategic decisions involve the ethereal aspects of organizational life and rely on the intuitive ways of knowing and understanding. Improvisation generally affects tactical decisions—defining ways and means—about how to reach goals and maintain the integrity of the organization.

Successful leaders are aware of the obvious and subtle dynamics of situations. They learn and know through data and intuition, develop the insight and foresight to read observable situations, and understand the fields and forces at play. They know when to change course to reach a goal and when to be creative, improvise, and break with convention ethically and with integrity. Steering the course to success may require ignoring plans, applying ingenuity, and improvising.

WHAT IS IMPROVISATION?

Improvisation is essential for leaders working in a perplexing and ambiguous milieu. Artists know and feel when it is time to break with convention and improvise. Leaders are not just strategists—they are also artists. Metaphorically, leaders are more like jazz musicians than they are like symphony conductors.

Symphony conductors help musicians interpret the music, its feeling, and its meaning. They rely on a written score with specific notes and dynamics that charts the plan for the music as defined by the composer. Certainly there are different interpretations; tempos may vary, but changing the themes, chords, dynamics, and notes is not in the score—the plan. Control of what is played and the sequence of themes and ideas rest with the composer.

Jazz musicians, however, have more latitude to create around the chords and themes in a piece. Jazz is not random noise or everyone doing his or her own thing. It has structure, discipline, and integrity based on the piece's chords. But, invention, creativity, and spontaneity are valued as musicians react to the moment and emotions in responding to the tune. Each musician may improvise in an individual way and still be in harmony with the overall meaning and feeling of the piece. Soloists create a mood—an aura—around the music that captures people's imagination and emotion.

Music is composed and structured around chords. Jazz musicians improvise on the basic structures of chords and melody, building on themes by taking a minimalist and subtle view or expounding on them in extreme, complex, or dramatic ways. They also play off the creativity of one another, responding to the improvised expression of colleagues. At times, there even may be collective improvisation as multiple players listen and react to one another or the soloist. They have a "conversation" around themes; they listen, they relate, they create, they innovate, they surprise, they extrapolate, they emote.

In all cases, the chords and tune set the stage and ultimate destination. Yet the chords, like corporate values and principles, allow for creative approaches, techniques, and methods to be implemented, while still preserving the integrity of the piece.

Jazz musicians build their musical path and solos around the chords in the music. In leadership, the principles and values are the footprints necessary for leaders to improvise and maintain integrity. With these, no step-by-step path or map is necessary. Our principles and values light the way and guide our creative reactions and impulses.

Improvisation has several key components and characteristics. Technique is important: understanding the processes, tools, and instruments and being agile in their application. Leaders must master the knowledge of "classic" and traditional approaches and processes and be skilled in implementing them in order to improvise on them. Knowing the discipline and content is required for skillful improvisation. Understanding techniques and rules is necessary if you are to improvise on them with integrity. In addition, intuition, synthesis, and creativity are indispensable to improvising.

Improvising in jazz includes embellishing on the theme and phrasing, and finding new patterns or motifs. Several approaches make these components effective:

- *When to play*—In music as in leadership there is a time to play and a time to rest. Pacing and silence become vital, as well as the quantity and nature of the activity. Too much playing can destroy the effect, and poor technique will not communicate. Silence is important because it gives the musical activity and sound impact. Constant noise, talking, or playing drowns out the message. Sometimes silence at the right time creates the effect that makes the sounds or words have monumental impact. Resting and reflecting can be powerful tools in creative leadership.

- *How to play*—Content and execution are very important and often are dependent on each other. Poor content excellently delivered is hollow. Great content poorly delivered is a waste. Leaders require wisdom and understanding, as well as the skills and strategies to deliver content with the right intent.
- *What to play*—The chords and melody form the basis for the embellishments, variations, and phrasing. Creative synthesis, fresh perception, and anticipation of what is emerging are important. Synthesis brings divergent ideas together, emphasizing connections and the application of ideas to new situations. Analysis, on the other hand, separates ideas into parts. In reacting to challenges, leaders need the power of ingenuity that synthesis brings. Great musicians and leaders can merge ideas—sometimes from different genres—and present them in surprising and inspired ways.

In jazz, as in leading, individual riffs are risky because they are very self-revealing, but they play on the outer edge of the known and create a sense of contribution and meaning. They can provide inspiration for the group to see new paths or instill a spark in them to try a new road. Improvising carries with it the risk of controversy and failure and second-guessing. Breaking ranks has the possibility of a breakdown, the responsibility for which rests directly on the shoulders of the leader.

IMPROVISATION: CONSTRUCTS AND DILEMMAS

> During periods of relaxation after concentrated intellectual activity, the intuitive mind seems to talk over and can produce the sudden insights, which give so much joy and delight.
>
> —Fritjof Capra

Contradiction is common in life, as are planning and improvisation. Just as adhering strictly to a plan can create failure, so can blind adherence to improvisation. Leaders need to understand when improvising is appropriate and must consider the following:

- *Bricolage*—Improvisation requires the skillful application of available resources to get the job accomplished, often with limited, insufficient, or different materials. Plans can get stifled due to inadequate materials, either because they are lacking in the first place or because there is not enough time to get them. Leaders improvise using available resources at hand to get the job done.
- *Intuition*—Great moments of dynamic tension call for all our faculties beyond rational logic. As beings, we are aware of things in ways other than through hard reason. We can feel and sense them. People act on things they know through all their faculties. Knowing means connecting the head with the heart and sensing what to act on and when to do it.

   Time is a factor in many decisions. Frequently judgments have to be made without hard, analytical data because it is not available, is not relevant, or cannot be obtained in a timely manner. In addition, the unseen forces at play can affect conclusions. Leaders with a deep knowledge of their jobs understand things without formal analysis and can make the intuitive choices necessary to achieve results. They know when to follow plans and when to modify them or deviate from them even though the formal data indicate otherwise.
- *Memory*—All leaders need knowledge, skills, and two types of memory to improvise. First, there is declarative knowledge—facts—from which they can make sense of the patterns they see. Second, leaders require procedural memory—the skills and routines to get things done. Procedural skills are needed to access knowledge so that appropriate and effective action can be taken. In a sense, declarative knowledge and procedural skills are the staples of traditional management.
- *Creativity and Learning*—Improvisation is a creative act. Innovative leaders know how to apply and customize procedural memory in novel ways or deviate from its normal application. There is a bit of trial and error to improvisation that can generate learning. By improvising, we may find new and more efficient ways to approach things, or we find out what does not work. In either case, we can be more effective.

How do you assess the impact of improvising? The first and essential question is: *Does improvising solve the problem*? To improvise for improvisation's sake is not the point. If it does not solve the problem then it is no better than pursuing rigid plans that cannot accommodate unknown and unforeseen factors.

Second, when we improvised, *did we create unexpected consequences that can reap great advantages?* Unanticipated opportunities may surface because a leader took a creative or an unexpected course. These opportunities may open doors to achievement not evident or available when we kept to the plan. In other words, we learn from improvising that can produce new productive approaches or shortcuts.

Third, *did improvising* destroy *the integrity of the organization?* Means do not justify ends. Selling out values and principles to achieve a worthy goal does irreparable harm and eventually devastates the value-driven behavior necessary for successful professional organizations. If the improvised approach cuts the legs out from under our values, then we should not use it. Improvisation requires integrity to principles and values—the chords.

IMPROVISING: DILEMMAS

- How do you create and maintain an organizational structure that allows spontaneity, creativity, and improvisation?
- How do you improvise without destroying the concepts and integrity of the plan?
- How do you improvise and maintain order in an organization?
- Can you create a strong, cohesive team and still have creative virtuosos?
- How do you balance individual autonomy with group or organizational needs?
- How do you create efficient systems that are also effective? How do you make music, rather than just play notes?
- How do you develop a creative organization and maintain the credibility of your basic values?

Fourth, *does improvising produce learning and provide a new or unique slant on an issue, causing people to think differently?* People incorporate innovative ways to achieve goals or to relate to one another when they see new possibilities. Improvising increases the capacity of people and organizations through experimenting, innovating, and learning from the experience.

Finally, *does improvising increase the efficiency of the organization by boosting the speed at which things get accomplished?* Through improvising, we sometimes learn that steps can be cut out of a process and we can still achieve our goals. Improvising can speed action. When time and resources are limited, this can be a great advantage. Increasing efficiency and effectiveness can save time and assets, and reduce pressure.

LEADERSHIP AND IMPROVISATION

Great leaders know how and when to improvise. They are disposed to achieving goals and helping people become more effective by building the capacity of people to respond to the unknown with motivation and skill. Improvisation requires nimbleness and flexibility, not tightness and rigidity.

Leaders, on the other hand, who inflexibly stick to plans and do not allow for deviation may cause damage. History is replete with leaders who were paralyzed in the depths of a well-conceived but ineffective plan. Strict adherence to impotent procedural plans in shifting times can produce frustration and failure. Blaming the environment or others for failure in the aftermath demonstrates a victim mentality. Leaders are not victims. They find ways to address the unexpected or the recalcitrant and move ahead. If failure is their companion, then it is not for lack of taking destiny into their own hands. Improvising requires risk. Hand-wringing and blaming are not in the cards.

The great jazz arranger Gil Evans had an orchestra that played at Sweet Basil, a jazz club in New York City, on Monday nights. Evans allowed for individual and collective improvisation in his musical arrangements. He defined the difference between a show and a performance. To Evans, a show was playing the same tunes the same way night after night. A performance, on the other hand, involved risk. Playing in the moment means approaching tunes in a new way, finding new paths, different nuances, and creatively showing another side to yourself and the music. A performance requires risk, while a show is stable and safely presents the same script, in the same sequence and the same manner. Venturing into new avenues and spontaneous creativity are not a part of a show.

To perform requires mastery of the discipline, craft, and technique that undergird the work—concepts, content, structures, processes. Knowing their work frees leaders to be tight around values and ethics but flexible around the application and aim of procedures. Values and principles set the limits for improvisation, acting like the chords in a jazz piece. They determine what improvisational approaches best fit the organization's culture and calling, and which ones are off limits. Leaders build a crucible of leadership in which professionals can use discretion and improvise in getting the job done while maintaining professional integrity, order, and ethical behavior. Leaders also are highly skilled at understanding tactics and are adept at customizing and using them to fit situations to successfully reach their goals.

Good improvisational leaders are also well grounded in both procedural and declarative knowledge. They have an intuitive sense of when to apply them. They do not just "wing it"—they combine the head and the heart, as well as art and science, to respond appropriately to situations.

The art of leadership is essential. While there are management techniques, data banks, and measurable indicators, leaders cannot run an organization with connect-the-dots processes. Leadership is not sticking to the "score," because statistics may not tell the whole story. Leaders have to respond absent complete information, requiring insight and "feel" in addition to hard data. Frequently, we don't have the time to gather all of the information in order to move ahead. Decisions have to be made. In crises, this is most evident, but these circumstances occur in other situations as well.

The art of leadership really rests on intangibles. Some musicians are highly technically proficient on their instruments but play with no emotional fervor or interpretative creativity. They play a string of notes; they don't make music. Complete professionals know the art and science of leadership, as well as matters of the heart and mind; this enables them to coalesce people around a common goal. We all know people who implement strategies capably but with no passion or fervor. They live in their heads and see everything as a cognitive exercise, and cannot connect on an emotional or spiritual basis.

Heart is important to accomplishment. Leaders need passion, creativity, and energy. They need persistence. They have to find a way to succeed against all odds. All are a part of improvising, using what you have, testing and piloting, and intuitively taking risks to adapt, adjust, and deviate.

The answer to leading and improvising lies in goals, values, and principles, the chords that allow improvisation with integrity. Improvisation is not reckless autonomy, and it is not people going their own way. And it is not dissonant noise—it is harmony with values and purpose.

PLANNING, PREDICTIONS, AND PROBLEMS

Great movements have "dynamic tension" between plans and circumstances and between adherence to set strategy and adapting to the unanticipated quirks of life. Leaders are leaders because they live for these moments and the challenges they present.

FAMOUS PREDICTIONS

The concept is interesting and well-informed, but in order to earn more than a "C," the idea must be feasible.

—A Yale University management professor in response to student Fred Smith's paper proposing a reliable overnight delivery service. Smith went on to found Federal Express.

With over fifty foreign cars already on sale here, the Japanese auto industry isn't likely to carve out a big slice of the U.S. market for itself.

—*Business Week*, August 2, 1968

There is no reason for any individual to have a computer in their home.

—Ken Olson, president, Digital Equipment Corporation, 1977

1930 will be a splendid employment year.

—U.S. Department of Labor, 1929

By the turn of this century, we will live in a paperless society.

—Roger Smith, chairman of General Motors, 1986

A severe depression like that of 1920–1921 is outside the range of possibility.

—Harvard Economic Society, November 16, 1929

They couldn't hit an elephant at this dist . . .

—General John B. Sedgwick, last words, Battle of Spotsylvania, 1864

SCENARIO PLANNING: BUILDING FUTURE MEMORY

The principal stood in front of the eighty-five staff members of her middle school and welcomed them to a new academic year. She indicated that the district's strategic plan had very important implications for their school, and she complimented the staff members who had spent time working on it with the consultants and the central district staff.

"Accountability today is high, and we must measure what we have accomplished using hard data, not speculation or opinions," she said enthusiastically. "There is a very important strategic goal for all schools concerning discipline. We want to reduce student discipline referrals to the office and suspensions by 15 percent over our benchmark total from last year. To gauge our progress, we will use the metric of the number of written referrals and suspension letters for in-school and out-of-school suspensions. The superintendent thinks all schools can meet this objective as we strive to improve discipline."

The teachers sat quietly; some glanced at one another, while others sat expressionless as the air in the room thickened. The principal looked around the room. The pause lingered heavily until Skip, the physical education teacher, raised his lanky arm. "Skip—do you have a comment or question?" the principal asked.

"Yeah, I guess I do," Skip said with a tone of reluctance in his voice. "The superintendent has been pushing strategic planning since he's been here. His salary bonus is tied to us meeting these strategic goals, and we are either viewed as a good or bad school depending on if we achieve them. But I've been thinking. We can make this a win-win for all of us," Skip said, warming up to his topic as he stood up and faced the staff. "We can give 'them' the numbers they need. All each one of us has to do is look away three times this year when we see a kid acting out. There are 85 of us, and if we ignore three behavior issues each, we will reduce referrals and suspensions by about 15 percent. The superintendent reaches his target. We reach our goal. We're considered a 'good' school. Everyone is happy. The sad thing is discipline will go to hell around here, and the kids will lose. Don't they understand that what you can measure with so-called metrics isn't always important or a true indication of a complex thing like school climate and discipline?"

Fiction? No. It is a real example from a "high-performing" school district in a metropolitan district in the Northeast. Strategic planning has taken school districts over the country by storm in the past decade. Consultants have made bundles helping school districts and state departments of education put their strategic goals into data-driven terms—setting benchmarks, establishing metrics, and determining measurable performance standards. But the best-laid plans can be circumvented by people or unexpected events. This is why those who put all of their stock in strategic planning and its data-laden processes have not changed schools or teaching dramatically.

The question is: What kind of planning is appropriate and for what purpose? Conventional wisdom and political correctness work against anyone raising questions about strategic planning. It is just assumed to be necessary, essential, and logical. Who wants to be a heretic? But there are pitfalls to any planning process, including strategic planning, and there is a mindset, a way of thinking and perceiving how the world works, behind each planning approach.

But in today's organizations, planning and getting the numbers are real forces, pressing leaders to behave in certain ways, sometimes out of convention, fear, or self-preservation.

The Polish poet Wislawa Szymborska, in the poem "A Word on Statistics," takes a satiric look at our penchant to apply numbers to everything in an effort to make it look more scientific and profound. In Western culture we worship at the altar of science, and the new priests are engineers and scientists, with their hard logic and columns of statistics. Szymborska writes:

Out of every hundred people

those of us who know better:
fifty-two.

Unsure of every step:
nearly all the rest.

Ready to help,
as long as it doesn't take too long:
forty-nine.

Always good,
because they cannot be otherwise:
four—well, maybe five.

Able to admire without envy:
eighteen.

Led to error
by youth (which passes):
sixty, plus or minus.

Those not to be messed with:
forty and four.

Living in constant fear
of someone or something:
seventy-seven.

Capable of happiness
twenty-some-odd at most.

Harmless alone,
turning savage in crowds:
more than half, for sure.

Cruel
when forced by circumstances:
it's better not to know
not even approximately.

Wise in hindsight:
not many more
than wise in foresight.

Getting nothing out of life but things:
thirty
(although I would like to be wrong).

Doubled over in pain,
without a flashlight in the dark:
eighty-three
sooner or later.

Those who are just:
quite a few at thirty-five.

But if it takes effort to understand:
three.

Worthy of empathy:
ninety-nine.

Mortal:
one hundred out of one hundred—
a figure that has never varied yet.[2]

Szymborska highlights the silliness of trying to place numbers on all facets of human behavior. Sometimes we think placing numbers on things make them seem more objective, credible, and important. But, as Szymborska expresses, there is only one statistic you can rely on—our certain mortality.

Our penchant for analyzing and calibrating everything sometimes gets out of hand or is not appropriate. As the old saw says, figures and numbers do not always tell the truth or picture reality. People drown in rivers that average three feet in depth. Our nation is poll crazy—trying to calculate everything from political aptitudes to perceptions of happiness. We have Likert scales for everything—as if my "five" were based on the same experience, criteria, or values as your "five." Is the distance between four and five the same for you and me? What is the metric for passion in music, for how much you love your spouse or partner, for your compassion, for your fears, for your fairness, or for your readiness to commit to a cause? While we try to place numbers on everything for comparisons and benchmarks, some things cannot be metrically analyzed and assessed. Sometimes people's intentions are not revealed by numbers. People can act the same but for different reasons and motivations.

One metric is certain in life. We are all mortal. But our spiritual and emotional essence cannot be measured. The depth of a person's heart and wisdom cannot be calculated by taking a test. Even IQ tests have been questioned—can one number really measure potential and intelligence?

The debate then becomes about objectivity and subjectivity. Our society believes numerical data is more objective, credible, and important than other data. There is a danger in the belief that putting a number on something makes for an objective assessment. Numbers appear so objective and charts so analytical. But they all can have a subjective twist—what numbers to report, how to report them, what questions to ask, what data are missing, and so on. Can the data be defended through research? If they are subjective, does that make them less credible? Can they be plotted and mapped? Can the numbers be used for planning? We certainly feel the satiric sting of trying to quantify all things, important and unimportant. For many aspects of human behavior quantitative statistics fall short.

Strategic planning has a place when problems require rational, linear, quantifiable, and data-driven approaches. But there are two problems with strategic planning. First, important things cannot always be measured and gauged with hard data. The world is a chaotic and inexplicable place; otherwise all of our plans would be immune to the butterflies whose small wing flutters create monumental windstorms. The second problem is that schools are people driven, complete with idiosyncrasies, intuition, hunches, beliefs, emotions, passion, free will, insight, spirit, biases, imagination, creativity, and a potpourri of other characteristics that are both infuriating and enduring. People are imaginative and unpredictable in both positive and negative ways, defying cause-and-effect planning and control.

Herein lies the argument for multiple or optional ways to plan. Forecasting, contingency planning, and strategic planning all have merit, but they are

---

He protects himself with the shield of science and the armor of reason. His enlightenment is born of fear; in the daytime he believes in an ordered cosmos, and he tries to maintain this faith against the fear of chaos that besets him by night.

—Carl Jung

premised on different assumptions and mindscapes. Projecting and forecasting enrollments, expenditures, revenues, time lines, and other things is useful in managing organizations. Looking through the rearview mirror of history to see where we have been and what was successful may have some virtue, providing people's behavior remains the same and the circumstances and events do not change too much.

The difficulty is: How can planning take into account the nonlinear, nonrational, emotional, and human aspects of life, society, and people? What are the tools to address a world filled with people who chase dreams, who believe in the impossible, who marvel at whimsy, and whose hearts move beyond logic and prediction?

Life is shaped by stories, with their unforeseen events and surprising endings, complete with twists and turns. Stories are imaginative and consider the small details and events that become marshaling forces, along with the subtle fields that move mountains. Through stories, we can think about the dynamics of the future. Poets write stories—about the past, about relationships, about dreams that recall the essentials of life and longing.

Life is a story that unfolds, and people's lives are stories that unfurl in intriguing ways, open to emotion, chance, and destiny. Obscure or accidental incidences or chords create great changes and repercussions. Synchronicity plays a part, as do the intangibles of belief, dreams, confidence, commitment, circumstance, and luck—good or bad.

Stories can move mountains. People relate to stories, and when you look at personal or organizational histories, stories develop in beautiful and startling ways. Stories, with all their human elements, can shed light on the future and cause us to reflect on the past and reveal wisdom. They have an emotional tenor that statistics lack.

Organizations, as living organisms, have stories too. Scenario planning offers leaders another planning approach, using plausible stories as a means to think about the future and to begin a dialogue about its prospects. These stories include factors that are obvious and manifest, but they also allow for what is not seen, but felt, and for invisible fields, spirit, and intangibles. Leaders engage in conversations with people, and scenarios can add richness and depth and move beyond graphs and charts in those conversations. If thought is a powerful system, then collective thought about the future through stories can help a desired future emerge.

Scenario planning offers leaders and policy makers another approach to planning in a world in which hard logic does not always prevail. Scenarios are not step-by-step strategies to get from point A to point B, nor are they linear, data-laden accountability procedures. Scenario planning is not just thinking about worse-case or doomsday scenarios. It offers the prospect of strategic *thinking* as a tool to deal with a world that is unpredictable and in which subtle and unseen fields affect people and society. Scenario planning can be coupled with other planning approaches to create a more comprehensive mosaic for what contemporary schools face.

SCENARIO PLANNING: WHAT IS IT?

Scenarios are not predictions, projections, or forecasts. Very simply, scenarios are credible stories about *plausible* futures that can be used as tools for strategic thinking and organizational learning.

Scenarios portray realistic, conceivable futures against which strategies and decisions can be played out. Scenario stories are not just willy-nilly speculation or science fiction. They are based around carefully constructed plots that address the *driving forces* and *predetermined elements* that, when combined with *critical uncertainties*, help define and structure plausible futures. These futures are not necessarily cloned pictures of the present. In fact, they may offer startling contrasts.

Driving forces are those social, economic, political, or technological undercurrents that affect and steer the trends and movements affecting our lives. Driving forces, some of which are unseen and under the surface, affect the major domains of our lives. For example, two evident driving forces today are technological advances that are engulfing our society and individuals' search for significance in their own lives. These two driving forces, while not directly at odds, present some interesting issues. Technologically empowered independence is available in the form of instant information, consumer options, and direct participation and involvement. At the same time people are searching for purpose in their lives amid the forest of information, material abundance, and frenzied pace of modern life. These two forces (and there are others) affect our economy, society, relationships, politics, priorities, and schools in concrete and intangible ways. They can create futures and mold our attitudes and thinking, and shape how we live, work, and relate. Leaders will have to be aware of how they might affect education and public schools, and be prepared to respond to them.

The second factor, *predetermined elements*, can more easily be defined because we can see evidence of them. They are inevitable, cannot be altered, and will influence the future. Demographics are one such predetermined element. Politicians, marketers, and educators are attuned to age cohorts so they can sell goods, craft political support, determine how and where to spend public dollars (e.g., schools or senior centers?), and assess the viability of social programs (e.g., social security).

The third component of scenarios, *critical uncertainties,* are those unpredictable issues that ride the waves of emotion, opinion, intuition, or chance. These are the things that drive planners crazy because they are not always obvious, rational, or logical. They are unexpected and cannot be calculated. Critical uncertainties shock us, at times, like firecrackers exploding in the dark. They are not predictable, and their impact may far outweigh their initial force. For example, consumer confidence cannot be predicted, because it is a critical uncertainty spawned by perception, belief, and emotion. Another example is the sudden and unanticipated resignation of an influential school board member over a matter of principle, or an unexpected attack by terrorists. Critical uncertainties create the mystery and exciting intrigue in the stories that unfold.

Even in the metrics-dominated field of economics there is a movement toward understanding the nonrational aspects of human behavior. The behavioral economics movement has made headway in this profession filled with data-driven economists and fueled by daily statistics, charts, and analyses.

The behavioral economists, who blend economics, psychology, and neuroscience, argue that emotion plays a huge role in people's economic decisions. Somehow, it seems surprising that some economists did not really understand that at the end of economic policy and statistical analyses are people—emotional beings who are not always rational and who may act on impulse. Otherwise, how do you explain fads and trends in fashions and entertainment?

The behaviorists feel that economics has been ruined by math. George Lowenstein, a professor at Carnegie-Mellon, believes that neoclassical economists wanted to mathematize the new science of economics. They could not, however, include any emotions or passions in their models, because emotions and passions are too unruly and complex. Lowenstein believes emotions affect matters in economics and all other segments of societal life.[3]

Emotions and passions are critical uncertainties that affect success in economics, life, and leadership. Emotion and passion, critical to great achievement or performance, are difficult to assess, but their impact moves the ordinary to the extraordinary and the mediocre to the exceptional.

Critical uncertainties add spice to scenarios and make them intriguingly different. If you do not believe critical uncertainties exist, look at politics, economics, marketing, popular culture, or any other facet of human endeavor. They are what cause people to say "Truth is stranger than fiction." While critical uncertainties are unpredictable, they can be influenced, just as public opinion, consumer confidence, or political credibility can, although without guaranteed effectiveness.

The components of driving forces, predetermined elements, and critical un-certainties are woven into plausible stories of what future(s) can unfold. Re-member, these scenario stories are not predictions: they are narratives that are plausible and encompass both linear and divergent thinking, logic and intu-ition, as well as rational and nonrational twists.

HOW SCENARIOS ARE USED

What does this have to do with leadership? Quite a bit. As planning tools, sce-narios are powerful. They present alternative images and possibilities, and because they are plausible and sometimes unnerving, they have the power to break stereotypes and generate "out-of-the-box" thinking. In a sense, they can give us a "whack on the side of the head" that produces insight and the "Aha!" experiences that produce ingenuity and new awareness.

Thinking is an essential key because it forms images, establishes what is possible, and defines our realities and prospects. Learning organizations think collectively, and scenarios are a critical force in helping people understand how different currents and dynamics may influence the future of public schools. As people think together, they must define their assumptions, evalu-ate them, and establish a collective understanding and common language. Scenarios do just that.

Scenarios provide a common vocabulary and the opportunity to engage in di-alogue—the process of collective thought—about each conceivable emerging future. Success in the future goes to the leaders who can determine what is *emerging*, not simply react to what is already manifested and obvious. Leaders must discern what is beginning to unfold down the road, because lightening-fast communication and instant and easy access to information is available to com-petitors and others. Scenarios, because they use linear, divergent, and intuitive thought processes, can provide insight into what may emerge when the driving forces, predetermined elements, and critical uncertainties converge.

Well-written scenario narratives can spur intuitive, as well as logical, ways of knowing—the rational and the nonrational sides of knowing and learning. Deep knowledge and sensitivity to conditions allow intuition to surface—our hidden voices that inexplicably provide insight in a way that is different from linear logic. Scenarios have room for those elements in life that are not quan-tifiable or tangible—the unobservable fields and forces at work in our lives and the universe that can have grand effects. These are the influences that linear-planning approaches miss. Scenarios not only can incorporate and con-sider what is not tangible and measurable, they can also apply those things to the issues raised in each scenario.

Scenarios can also lead to what Royal Dutch Shell Oil executive Arie de Geus called "future memory." By thinking strategically about possible emerging futures, leaders can consider and test their assumptions and play out possible decisions, thereby gaining some "future memory" if those plausible scenarios come to pass. In other words, scenarios can create "practice" for leaders and managers and then, if confronted by the situation, they will have some "memory" as to what options and alternatives might be successful in meeting the challenges. This can reduce reaction time and assist in the future with decision making, consensus, and understanding.

In effect, scenarios provide an early warning signal of what might be unfolding, determine the competence of professionals and leaders in the system to face new challenges, generate better strategic options, develop future memory, and evaluate the risk return of the various strategic options.

David Bohm, the British physicist, philosopher, and protégé of Einstein, indicated that thought is a system that can affect the implicate order of the universe.[4] Looking at the universe through strictly part-to-whole thinking that relies on calculable hard data may not be sufficient in a complex world. Determining what is emerging—what is not already evident—keeps schools and other organizations viable in an ever-changing context. Scenarios add a healthy dimension to planning that includes the immeasurables of life that consistently surprise us and shatter our linear, strategic plans. Scenario planning is a complimentary tool for leadership and strategic decision making in a chaotic and uncertain future.

It is June and the faculty is meeting to review the year. "Congratulations," the principal says. "I am pleased to announce that we met all of our goals in the strategic plan." She smiles and looks around the room. "Concerning discipline, our referrals and suspensions were reduced by 16.9 percent over last year. The superintendent is very pleased."

Skip sat quietly, reflecting on the year. The goals had been met, yet there was no sense of satisfaction. There was a gnawing in his chest that betrayed the success reflected in the numbers.

"I hate to ruin the party," Skip blurted out, surprising even himself. "Sure, the numbers look good. But, we lost something. Schools aren't businesses, kids aren't customers, and the bottom line is not a batch of statistics. We've been so focused on reaching our so-called measurable goals and making ourselves look good, we're losing what made this school special. Some of you don't like to hear this, but we're great at the 'political game' of schooling and the so-called metrics, but we're losing the human connection between teacher and student," Skip continued with increasing passion.

"Schools are sanctuaries for children, where they can learn, make mistakes, and find out about themselves and the world. When we focus so hard on numbers—test scores, attendance, data—we lose sight of the kids and their total development. We're in danger of making major issues minor, and minor issues major. What data show our commitment or if our classes are exciting, creative places? We're focusing on statistics, forgetting that there's an art, a human element, in what we do too. Remember the great teachers in your lives? Their passion and compassion weren't rooted in numbers. Well, enough of my venting—this pseudoscientific data stuff really frustrates me."

Skip sat down, then quickly bolted up and said, "One more thing. This may be a cheap shot, but we do the work and the superintendent gets the big-buck bonus. What did he do to get the numbers? We hardly saw him here all year!"

NOTES

1. Collins, Billy. "Butterfly Effect," in *Sailing Alone Around the Room*. New York: Random House, 2001, p. 151.

2. Szymborska, Wislawa. *Miracle Fair*. New York: Norton, 2000, p. 99.

3. Kopcke, Richard, Jane Snedden Little, and Geoffrey M. B. Tootell. "How Humans Behave: Implications for Economics and Economic Policy." *New England Economic Review*, first quarter, 2004, p. 16.

4. Bohm, David. *Wholeness and the Implicate Order*. New York: Routledge, 1980.

8

Leadership, Calling, and Spirit

Listen, are you breathing just a little, and calling it a life?

—Mary Oliver

Why do you want to lead? Why did you want to assume a position of leadership? These are two fundamental questions. Is it to complete your resume? Is it ego? Is it a matter of expectations—yours or others? Is it about power and authority? These questions matter to the people who are led, but they also are of prime importance to the person leading. What is the drive to lead?

Leadership is important in all of our lives—personally, professionally, and nationally. Why people become leaders is important to ponder as much as how people behave as leaders. The two are intertwined. The principles that call people to positions of leadership are vital because they focus perspectives and vision. The principles on which we lead define how we will behave and relate to others and what we want to accomplish.

At times, people see leadership through rose-colored glasses. They begin to believe that style will supercede substance, and that image and appearance are at the core of leadership. Look good. Dress well. Play the part. Rely on charisma. They personalize the position so that it is synonymous with the person holding it.

Style cannot overwhelm a lack of substance. Too frequently we fall prey to charisma and the cult of personality. While style is engaging, when organizations face dire issues, style falls mute in the cacophony of crisis. The "empty suit" syndrome is about hollowness dressed up in appearances. Leadership is about principle, not personality.

Leaders have a style unique to themselves that is reinforced by substance. Style alone leads to serious problems because it can be manipulative and vested in ego. The cult of personality also broadcasts that there are "special" people who deserve to be leaders, under the assumption that there is an inherent destiny for some to lead through connections, birthright, fame, or fortune. If leadership is based on the concept of specialness, then it becomes divisive. If leaders are special, then we, the people, are not. Specialness produces separation and distance.

The concept of distance is important in leadership. As Heraclitus said: "Dogs bark at everyone they don't know."[1] The extent to which specialness increases the distance between leaders and followers is the extent to which their legitimacy is compromised: the greater the distance, the less the credibility, and, conversely, the smaller the distance, the greater the credibility.

The more distant leaders are from the people with whom they work, the greater the chance of failure; the less distance, the greater the chance of success. Distance is not about physical or geographical space. It is really about substance and relationships that either build believability or produce "straw dogs" pretending to be leaders.[2] Integrity, when it is evident to people, closes distance. Without integrity credibility is lost, and without credibility leaders lose the ability to lead.

Leaders should strive to minimize the distance between the following factors:

- *Words and Behavior*—Words and actions must be in harmony and must be congruent for leaders to reduce distance and build standing and trust. Without those qualities people will not put their efforts and beliefs on the line. They will not follow.
- *Values and Processes*—Organizations with integrity have processes that are in accord with their values. The ends do not justify the means. Machiavelli does not live in the leader's office.
- *Experience and Learning*—Organizational learning is important. Some initiatives will not be successful: Will people learn from mistakes and failures? Or is catching people in mistakes the norm?
- *Goals and Outcomes*—Reaching desirable goals is important for the organization to be convincing. Feeling good and not accomplishing things becomes vacant and self-defeating. Leadership is not about leaders; it is about achieving significant things.
- *Relationships and Authenticity*—Leaders who lack sincerity will not be "real" or authentic in relationships, and people will know it. Being comfortable with people, not being ego driven, and actively listening to people are essential.

In politics, particularly, we listen cynically to candidates, who share words that ring true and then often do something totally alien or nothing at all. We hear of noble ideas and then experience bankrupt procedures and policies, devoid of coherence and principle. We hear the bugle call of great goals and then experience a paucity of resolve or hollow achievement. We hunger for realness and genuineness in our leaders and are disappointed when we find phoniness and posturing. We yearn for relationships built on trust and straight talk and tire when they dissolve into condescension and glibness.

The promise of talent falls on the barren, rocky soil of ego and arrogance, as some leaders lack the courage to admit failure and to learn from it. To them, appearances and posturing are greater virtues than success. The Brahmins, who live above the fray of everyday life and believe that they should inherent power, eventually lose the very authority necessary to lead. Leadership is more than role-playing, just as it is more than the processes and practices we learn in graduate school.

Graduate schools teach about leadership: sometimes in a vacuous, antiseptic manner divorced from the personal stake, relationships, and intangible connections that leaders need to make. Lessons look like exercises in engineering. Just place the proper procedures in the proper sequence and you too can lead. Making a decision? Just collaborate and get the "stakeholders" vision. Got a political problem? Just join the Rotary Club and "network." Have a student achievement problem? Put standards in place and mine data for the solution. It all seems so simple, as if anyone can do it if they only held the title and position. People lead: procedures and data do not.

We teach the "doings" of leadership—processes we have all learned going back to scientific management, management by objectives, reengineering our organizations, standards-based leadership, and any mutation thereof. PERT (planning, evaluation review technique) charts from the space shuttle era, and the litany of planning, organizing, staffing, directing, coordinating, reporting, and budgeting (POSDCORB) still ring in the ears of people who want to produce results strictly through systems.

These "doings," which are not devoid of value if placed in the proper perspective, are empty in terms of getting people to coalesce around a common objective in a complex socio-emotional-political-economic environment. Deep commitment is not born in the power of analysis, data, and statistics.

Contemporary thought and initiatives assert that we live in the age of information. We have even created information technology departments, complete with directors and managers. Information is king. David Whyte, in his poem "Loaves and Fishes," states that people hunger for more, and that information alone is not a high enough standard to cause people to commit their lives.

This is not
the age of information.

This is *not*
the age of information.

Forget the news,
and the radio,
and the blurred screen.

This is the time
of loaves
and fishes.

People are hungry,
and one good word is bread
for a thousand.[3]

Data and information, while useful, do not have the power to capture people, to have them serve, to have them commit their potential and talent, or to have them dedicate their lives. People are hungry for something greater than computer printouts, graphs, regression analyses, and tests of statistical significance. Dee Hock, the father of the universal Visa credit card said: "We are drowning in a raging flood of new data and information, and the raft of wisdom to which we desperately cling is breaking up beneath us."[4] Data and information are limited, and low in the taxonomy of understanding. Sometimes the data and information are not correct—they require the intuition and wisdom to interpret only human beings can provide. People yearn to live lives of significance, and they look beyond statistics to find meaning and wisdom and relationships that really matter. Reaching beyond self and mundane numbers to noble ideals nourishes us—inside and outside. It provides significance to our desire to be stewards.

Leadership is about "being," not only "doing." Meister Eckhart, the German mystic theologian, stated: "It is not by your actions that you will be saved, but by your being. It is not by what you do, but by what you are that you will be judged."[5] The vein of gold in leadership is about who we are as leaders.

Our being speaks louder than our words. "Being" has to do with authenticity, our values, integrity, beliefs, and humor. Essentially it is about being the person we are with our heads, hearts, spirit, and souls. "Being" is about genuineness, truth, and essence, not about style and appearances. When we are "being" we live in the here and now, not in the past or the future: we are "being" in the moment.

Our being is not tied to ego or "having" things or titles, but it is concerned with who we are; it allows us to take risks and endure criticism in hard times, and not bow to "losing" position, power, or possessions. We want to *have* power, position, control, and success, and, consequently, our lives are centered on things and roles, and not people. Having is geared to possessing and owning. We even ask "Who owns this problem?" and "Does he/she possess the skills or talent?" People also want to "have" security. Risks and doing what is "right" may fall prey to the desire to hold on to the social status that we "have."

When we own things, we crave them, and our ego and self-interest are wrapped into them. We want to hold on to things we have, including intangibles like respect, loyalty, and satisfaction. Trying to motivate people through material goods (cars, fringes, bonuses, trips, etc.) is part of this "having" mentality.

> To be what we are, and to become what we are capable of becoming, is the only end of life.
>
> —Robert Louis Stevenson

A key question is: Should leaders *be* authorities or should they *have* authority by virtue of their position? Being an authority has a rational aspect to it, because it is based on competence and assumes that the person is wise enough and has a highly developed expertise and is a polestar or person of significance. Having authority, on the other hand, is based on hierarchal position and social status. Would you want a physician who was to perform surgery on your eyes to be an authority on such surgery, or would you want him or her to simply have the authority to perform it?

Our unique being communicates more than we know. Commitment can come from exuberance, but it also lives in calm resolve. Leadership can sail on the wings of charismatic figures, but it also can travel on the quiet intensity and passion of calling and love. Talent can define promise, but ability devoid of wisdom is dangerous. The call to serve can occur through the call of bugles or it can come through the reflection of calling. How we are as beings and how we create relationships determines whether we can capture people's passion to make a commitment to the collective goal.

Some see leadership as the power to control and direct using image and processes. Others see power as the energy of potential, commitment, and the potential of ideas and thought.

NOBLE IDEAS AND POWER

Ideas and thought are very forceful, and both are critical to successful leadership. What we think becomes who we are, and, as a consequence, it is essential to consider how leaders think.

Leaders are conceptual thinkers who see the world in complex ways and understand how people and purpose connect. They often see shades of gray and they can live with ambiguity and uncertainty because they do not expect the world to be an orderly and tidy place composed of black or white questions. Confusion is tolerable because change occurs with disequilibrium and its resulting residue of unanticipated outcomes. Disconfirming data and information are accepted, as these leaders adjust their thinking and possibly disregard past practice. Leaders transform and help others transform organizations through values, ideas, and principles.

Physicist David Bohm asserts that there is a potential problem with thinking—fragmentation.[6] We frequently break our world into discrete bits and pieces. Our approach to thinking is not holistic—instead, we go from component to component. Organizations are based on this mind frame. As we break our world into isolated pieces, we create phalanxes of specialists and divide ourselves as a nation into groups of hyphenated citizens.

Systems thinking considers organizations as interconnected, dynamic, evolving, and developing integral entities. The scientific method emphasizes analysis—slicing a problem, issue, or thing into parts, which is a fragmented approach. Holistic thought, however, examines complete entities and examines the forceful and subtle dynamics that affect conditions and the web of interconnections and relationships. The integral nature of things and their subtle interconnections have great consequences.

Our thoughts are not isolated from how we perceive our total being. Through fragmented thinking we see our mind as where thought resides, our body as where our physical being is housed, and our emotions as where our feelings are contained. But we are not that discreet. Our thoughts affect our feelings and can create physical conditions. Our physical health affects our emotions and thinking. We are a whole being, integrally connected through head, heart, and spirit—all interwoven and inseparable. We are not simply a conglomeration of parts.

How we think is important because it permeates everything we do and how we do it. In essence, thought creates our world and our own reality: it is not just benign or philosophical pondering, because we act on it. Bohm states that how we think produces some of the very problems we wish to solve. He states: "The tendency to produce conflict comes from our thought. . . . The way of thinking has a name: fragmentation. The word fragment means to smash, to break up."[7] Bohm believes that fragmented thinking creates separation, and he uses the word *smash* to indicate that the whole cannot be put back together again. Fragments can lead to illusions, and illusions can lead to conflict and confusion.

Trying to remain aware of the whole and not simply analyze parts is difficult, because leaders have traditionally been trained to analyze parts through the scientific method and management approaches.

Fragmented thinking is evident in our organizations, with their emphasis on structure and departments, functions and responsibilities, and roles and responsibilities. Knowledge is disjointed and can become dangerous, as the competition between divisions and departments of the American intelligence services clearly demonstrates.

In schools today we also have focused on structures and standards and the constant metrical analysis of the parts. If we collect data on skills and concepts we think we will understand the health of the whole. We study variables as if they were separate and distinct, trying to identify the ones that will cause the others to react in positive ways. For example, we search for one statistically significant variable that leads to great increases in students' standardized test results.

Fragmented thinking leads to strong boundaries and separation. The impetus for change becomes stymied by these boundaries because they protect the stability and security of the people working in the department. These boundaries build safety from the external world and thwart leaders who try to change them. The inertia of separateness becomes dominant, unless leaders find a different way for people to think about organizations and their interconnected relationships.

Margaret Wheatley, in her book *Leadership and the New Science* indicates,

> Power in organizations is the capacity generated by relationships. How leaders organize relationships is more important than how functions and tasks are organized. The energy from tight relationships is the power that can break inertia because people are really "bundles of potential" that, if capitalized, can change the world. Listening, sharing stories, and eliminating the boundaries that separate us can bring out the power of energized people working together in a common enterprise.[8]

We can build a perceptual prison. If we see our world as we always have, our behavior will remain the same. As one teacher, who was given the latitude to help a committee redesign his school, said, "I can't think of doing anything any differently because this is all I know. I can't think about it any other way." He personifies the adage, "If you do what you've always done, you'll get what you've always gotten."

Leaders shake up people's perceptions of and thinking about their world. Ideas capture the imagination, stir creativity, and excite the spirit: all activities of the soul. The power of ideas is fundamental to efforts aimed at changing and producing schools with a sense of goodness. Ideas, particularly noble and important ones, form fields of thought, which generate energy and motivation that establish new structures and processes. Unfortunately, ideas are viewed as esoteric or philosophical and are not always seen or understood as a catalyst for change. What is more pragmatic, however, than an idea?

Ideas and the "force fields" around them can help people see the integral nature of concepts because they produce power and dialogue. Ideas help people make sense of the uncertainty and ambiguity with which they struggle. Concepts provide a framework for us to understand confusion, or at least help us think about it in a productive way without being immobilized.

How leaders think is not an insignificant thing and has both a bright and a dark side. We hunger to get inside leaders' heads to better understand them, their motives, and their actions. As leaders, we must look at ourselves and see the shadows that can affect our thinking and actions. Parker Palmer states:

> Leadership is hard work for which one is regularly criticized and rarely rewarded, so it is understandable that we need to bolster ourselves with positive thoughts. But by failing to look at our shadows, we feed a dangerous delusion that leaders too often indulge: that our efforts are always well intended, our power is always benign.[9]

The delusions Palmer refers to are figments of our imagination that form a mindscape that can be destructive and produce dark-side leaders.

THE DARK SIDE OF LEADERSHIP

Leadership has a bright side, filled with optimism and wonder, but it also has a dark side—an underbelly that feeds on fear, cynicism, and mistrust.

> Anger, fear, aggression—the dark side of the Force are they.
>
> —Yoda, *Star Wars*

When people wonder why schools are ineffective or reform fails, the "dark side" may be at work. Just as in the movie *Star Wars*, this dark side is fueled by anger, fear, and aggression.

Leaders hate to admit that these factors exist in their organizations and professional lives. Darth Vaders can turn positive climates and conditions and attempts at fundamental change into grim and futile experiences. To lead successfully, we must honestly recognize the dark side and understand the rules that govern it.

The Darth Vaders are characters we have all experienced. They are in the formal organizational structure, using authority and power for negative purposes—to intimidate and oppress. They live in informal interactions and relationships, too; although less obvious here, they are very potent, especially when innovation and change are proposed. These negative characters also appear in the external environment, in political or special interest groups that try to gain control through deception, character assassination, and mistrust.

The dark side needs to be exposed so the positive advocates can grasp the pressures and influences they must counteract to achieve success. While Darth Vaders stalk the halls of all organizations, there is also the bright side—leaders who fight for goodness, virtue, and constructive change and who do not surrender to the dark side of cynicism and pessimism. Instead, they pursue values, high purpose, and integrity and work to abolish fear, anger, and uncertainty.

> To live is to choose. But to choose well, you must know who you are and what you stand for, where you want to go and why you want to go there.
>
> —Kofi Annan, secretary general of the United Nations

Gandhi knew of both the bright and the dark side of life and leadership. He feared that the trappings and perquisites of position could seduce leaders. He said:

> Man must choose either of the two courses: the upward and the downward; but as he has the brute in him, he will move more easily to choose the downward course than the upward, especially when the downward course is presented to him in beautiful garb. Man easily capitulates when sin is presented in the garb of virtue.[10]

ELEMENTS OF THE DARK SIDE

Dark-side leaders know how to use fear, anger, and aggression to frustrate processes, to contain thinking, and to intimidate those who try to change. They are driven by ego and use the gravity of custom to support the status quo. Egocentricity focuses on the power of personality, not ideas or the common good. These leaders reject ideas that threaten their self-interest and weaken their illusion of control, and they undermine any change that does not work to their benefit. Self-protection and security are the goals, because these leaders see new ideas from other sources as threats to themselves and their status.

Dark-side leaders who are threatened use formal and informal coercive power. In these power relationships, people are dehumanized into roles and titles and not perceived as individuals. Resisting ideas from a role or position is easier than opposing a real person, with a personality, feelings, and needs. These intimidating power relationships depersonalize people and create stereotypes based on position or title, making resistance and abuse easier because the negativism is targeted at impersonal positions and titles. Opposing ideas is also easier when they came from "downtown," the "ivory tower," "management," "those liberal department chairpersons," or "union teachers" rather than from specific individuals with names, faces, and histories. Depersonalizing the debate gives dark-side leaders license to use any tactic, ethical or not, to maintain current conditions or to serve egocentric purposes by creating a "we-they" mentality.

For people to become fearful, there does not have to be a real threat—just the perception of one. Fear drives out logic and love, and creates panic and anxiety that can stymie people and destroy relationships. Dark-side leaders thrive on illusions. When people confront the uncertainty of new ideas or the insecurity of change, the fertilization and incubation of fearful illusions is easy and has a great effect.

Fear germinates from the anxiety of uncertainty or of faulty or scarce communication. Then, creating illusions that go far beyond the realm of reality is easy and jeopardizes security. People become insecure and they create scenarios around their worst fears; they take their nastiest imaginings and explode them into dire predictions. In most things in life, our worst fears never play out. Things are not as bad as we think, and silver linings and opportunities do appear in times of trial. With illusions, however, there are no silver linings: just gloom and doom.

Dark-side leaders paint negative delusions by coloring perceptions, attributing false motives to others' actions, and creating dastardly scenarios. Perceptions affect how people think about things and eventually how they act. When perception is controlled, thought is directed and influenced. Fearful perceptions generate frightful thoughts, which result in fight-or-flight behavior. That is why dark-side leaders begin early and try to influence the perceptual screens through which people process data and information.

Another dark-side strategy is the shadow of *attribution*, which fixes reprehensible motives to the individuals or people advocating a particular idea. People will resist even good ideas if the implication is spread that they are implemented for evil motives. People will shy away from other people who are characterized in negative and objectionable ways. Character assassination is effective in politics for that very reason. The allegation may be made that if new ideas and precedents are tried, then all hell will break loose; or ideas that are said to sound good may be prostituted into negatives. Or the old saw "Consider the source" may derail people's efforts and turn off thoughtful reflection.

Finally, shadowy scenarios may be projected that play on the fears or ambiguity associated with change in the status quo. What change in life does not carry uncertainty? Ambiguity is fertile soil for rumors, doomsday projections, and wild illusions, complete with nightmare endings. These scenarios usually portend disaster for the welfare and status of specific groups or individuals.

THE RULES OF THE DARK SIDE

Several dark-side rules must be either neutralized or overcome if schools are to be sanctuaries for children and learning and places where people can fulfill themselves. The aim of these rules is to control behavior through fear and anxiety.

Rule 1: Use fear as a major weapon to maintain conformity to current practice.

Fear—of retribution, discipline, or isolation—is a tool to move employees to behave in certain ways. All of these tools deal with loss. Fear does not motivate people, but it does activate them to do something through force or pressure, not from internal motivation, high purpose, or inspiration. Guns, for example, can move people to do things, but they are not motivators. They are blatant examples of instruments of coercive fear and external control that can move people to do things against their will. The fear of losing a job can have the same power.

While fear resides deep in the formal structures of bureaucracies and autocratic leadership, there is fear among peers, too. Informal groups can create tyranny and intimidation through peer sanctions, which, while subtle, are sometimes more potent than formal retribution. Any teacher who has been "iced" by colleagues understands the impact that social isolation has on self-esteem and confidence. Being isolated emotionally and intellectually is most harsh because it makes the person feel deficient and even subhuman if the intensity is great enough. The fear of intellectual isolation is very subtle. Individuals who do not operate based on conventional wisdom are at risk of being quarantined. Despite the cry for academic freedom, people cannot stray too far from the beaten path of accepted practice or ideas. Being out of the mainstream can leave some teachers "up the creek," disconnected from relationships with colleagues. Tolerance for different ideas is not a value that is strongly entrenched when bureaucratic culture dictates otherwise.

People need to be connected to others, and withholding that contact is brutalizing because the necessity for professional respect and approval is a very dominant one. Leaders and others fear losing their credibility with their peers, and some will do anything to maintain acceptance, even if it means selling out their values and "souls."

Fear also gives birth to standardism—jargon for the "We've always done it this way" mentality. There is no risk in maintaining the status quo because it validates current skills and knowledge. In contrast, innovation creates uncomfortable situations in which present expertise may not match new situations or expectations. Professional reputations are rooted in competence, and any change that requires new knowledge or skills threatens them. Fear of the unknown implications of change causes anxiety, which, in turn, may result in a fight-or-flight response. The active or passive aggression created by fear can effectively blunt reform efforts, maintain the status quo, or reduce innovation to mere tinkering.

Fear is inversely related to the level of trust and openness in the system. Closed systems, characterized by restricted internal and external communication and influence, have less trust and more apprehension about new ideas because there is a price to pay for making mistakes, assuming responsibility, or raising issues. Open systems, with good communication between people, foster trust and allow for mistakes, new ideas, and free expression. Conversation and dialog cannot take place in a closed system, and, therefore, it plants the seeds of failure and lost innovation.

Rule 2: Use informal power structures to supersede formal ones and stymie change efforts.

Informal power can be more trenchant and intimidate with more potency than formal control, since formal sanctions are specified and defined. There are rules in contracts and laws for the application of formal sanctions, complete with due process safeguards. The dark side of peer power carries no such constraints. It can determine what issues are raised, establish deference to informal leaders, and restrict speech and action by eliminating professional autonomy and promoting conformity. Informal power brokers are obsessed that their influence will be jeopardized. Therefore, they resist innovation or independence and they work behind the scenes—using people's desire to be "in" and not "out" of their peer group, and feeding off the mistrust individuals have of the formal power structure.

Informal power can require conformity to norms and standards of behavior. Just as there is politically correct language, there is pedagogical correctness in schools. Pedagogical correctness pushes people to stay with traditional teaching, organization of classes, delivery of curriculum, performance assessment, and scheduling of students. When some teachers attempt new approaches, they are sanctioned and informally coerced back into line. Breaking precedent and trying new ideas sparks suspicion and criticism, because established routines are valued as the "standard," and new ways are reduced to cynical degradation.

A related issue is "group shift," which is also caused by the pressure and need to be accepted and the fear of isolation. People make more extreme decisions in groups than they might alone. People do things in groups that they would find repulsive individually. The direction of the group dominates individual perception and thinking. Members deflect responsibility and rationalize decisions, even though they may have qualms about them. Standing against colleagues takes courage because if people do not "go along," they can be castigated socially.

Dark-side formal or informal leaders poison the well of innovation by undermining the motives, procedures, and outcomes of reforms. The dark side appeals to individuals who thirst for personal power and who want to maintain their comfort and status.

Rule 3: Say you want progress, but work to maintain the status quo and frustrate change.

Change is an abstraction, but the status quo is a reality. People are comfortable advocating change but are uncomfortable actually changing. The rhetoric of reform is more dramatic than prescriptions for change. According to conventional orthodoxy, for change to be accepted it must be modest and built on current structures. The seedlings of change must be small, with lengthy periods of time provided for them to take root. In other words, comprehensive change is perceived as bad: the less significant the change, the better.

When reform is proposed, several dark-side tactics are used to frustrate it. A common one is sending the change back to a planning committee for more work and investigation. Planning is always a good excuse for inaction; it seems so rational that it is difficult to dispute, and it suffocates innovation with excessive organizing. Another tactic is the use of hyperbole that is intended to muster alarm by labeling the change radical. As in politics, name-calling, sound bites, and labeling are potent excuses for not thinking. Understanding a complex or comprehensive proposal is more work than simply attaching a negative, sensational label to it. Well-placed rumors also serve this purpose. For example, if a proposal is designed to reduce high-stakes testing, then "lack of standards" is alleged and charges of fostering mediocrity are proclaimed. The dark side sometimes leaps from inside schools to the editorial pages of newspapers, through rumors and half-truths, to manipulate public opinion.

The environment surrounding schools also has a dark side, which adds a complicating dimension. Dark-side leaders who operate in this external world can affect the climate inside of schools. Their appeal is the same—fear and anger. Whether perpetrated by dominating leaders or special-interest power groups, external dark-side strategies are the same as those used inside. The external environment is frequently driven by politics, complete with power struggles and "hard-ball" tactics. External dark-side strategies seek to influence public opinion through distortion, oversimplification, and confusion.

The "big lie," a staple in politics, is a weapon frequently used in organizations. The strategy is simple: take an idea and through a gross, distorted application move it to a radical extreme. The idea is taken out of context and put in opposition to traditional values or concepts, and the advocates are placed in disrepute through ridicule or name-calling. Derision and sarcasm are key ingredients, coupled with a healthy dose of smug indignation. The proponents of the idea are left trying to defend an outlandish position and clarifying a raft of misrepresentations and oversimplifications. The blizzard of misquotes and perversions creates panic in the community and impugns the reputation of the idea's advocates. As political heat boils and the issue polarizes the community, policy makers shy away from it and try to disarm the controversy through abandonment or compromise.

THE BRIGHT SIDE OF LEADERSHIP

Leadership is a sacred concept, carrying with it unique responsibilities and obligations. Great leaders have a profound impact through the innate desire of people to use their abilities for noble purposes.

While we all admire the great leaders who have dotted history or those with whom we have worked, there are others who have led in negative and destructive ways. These people squander their talents and opportunities as leaders, and the consequences of their leadership are littered throughout the centuries— Hitler, Stalin, and McCarthy are striking examples of leadership from the dark side. These "bad seeds" distort and pervert the obligations of leadership.

These dark-side leaders appeal to base instincts by preying on people's fears, prejudices, and dependencies. One tactic is manipulating communication that intentionally muddles issues by oversimplifying, distorting, or confusing. The natural anxiety people have when trying something new or facing difficult times is exploited by these methods. They heighten anxiety and nurture fear of the unknown, thereby short-circuiting ideas before they have a chance to be considered thoroughly and discussed openly. Mindsets get established, and the discussion of change begins with negative assumptions and perceptions.

> The right team, creating the right communities and businesses, by doing the right thing.
>
> —Bonita Bay Group, Bonita Bay, Florida

Fearful people are susceptible to stereotypes that can feed on deep-seated prejudices. For example, in the past when schools were being integrated, some dark-side leaders indicated that academic standards would be compromised and that schools would be less safe. Frightened people find reasons for maintaining the status quo, and the seemingly respectable concern for standards masks the anger underlying the situation. Members of the dark side frequently obscure negative motives under the veil of noble ideals.

Dark-side leaders create dependence. The bright side exalts individual talent and potential, seeing people as basically good. Given a commitment to strong values and noble purposes, people will do the right things if they have the support, autonomy, and discretion to do so. But some leaders do not want independent people; they need dependent employees whose behavior is contingent on the leader's approval. This dependence is the ultimate celebration of ego, and it destroys individual growth and limits the potential of the school. Dark-side leaders like dependence because it satisfies their ego needs and keeps power and control in their hands.

Finally, charismatic dark-side leaders without a strong ethical core can be destructive. The force of personality can be intoxicating and appealing. Hitler's mesmerizing speeches, coupled with his personality, won him a cult of followers, even though his message was morally corrupt and appealed to dark prejudices and hatred. This same thing can happen in communities and organizations. The charisma of the person and the attraction of personality can be destructive if the person's soul is not connected to positive values or norms.

Leadership carries great obligations and the bright side of optimism. It is frustrating, at times, and defeat may be part of the package. As Teddy Roosevelt said, "Far better is it to dare mighty things, to win glorious triumphs, even though checkered by failure, than to take rank with those poor spirits who neither enjoy much nor suffer much because they live in the gray twilight that knows not victory nor defeat."[11] Roosevelt was from the bright side: he honored the human spirit for accepting challenges, rejecting the fear of failure, and attempting to make things better.

When we let ego's shadow emphasize our dark sides, we as leaders can get into serious trouble. Palmer indicates, "When I ignored my own truth on behalf of a distorted ego and ethic, I led a false life that caused others pain—for which I can only ask forgiveness."[12]

The poet Szymborska, in "Our Ancestors' Short Lives," addresses the relationship between good and evil—the bright and dark sides.

> Good and evil—
> they knew little of them, but knew all:
> when evil triumphs, good goes into hiding;
> when good is manifest, then evil lies low.[13]

Leaders appeal to the best in people's desires, motives, and instincts. Goodness is a very powerful force coming from our souls. Leadership is about poetry, not process. It comes from the head and heart and venerates the human spirit. Leadership tied to the organization's soul—high professional performance and moral purpose—can defeat contemptible appeals to the dark side of human nature.

In essence, the purpose of leadership is to liberate the human spirit to do the right things and meet the responsibilities and obligations of our profession. Leaders must be moored to high values and model them in word and deed. They cannot mouth one set of values and live another in their decisions and practice. They must express outrage and take difficult and sometimes unpopular stands when their values and ethical standards are violated.

The dark side exists in each of us as we face the uncertainties of change and challenges to our attachments. Inherent in each individual, however, is the bright side that can shelter and nurture us in times of doubt: the bright side of love, compassion, forgiveness, truth, and justice. A concern for the commonweal—the benefit of all—is inherent in what schools are to be if children and teachers are to meet their potential in difficult times. Leaders must understand the dark side and use the spirit of goodness to take on the courageous act of leading toward the light—the bright side.

LEADERSHIP: A PERSPECTIVE

Leaders are people who try to work for the common good in a sense of stewardship. Leadership is not simply cognitively solving a complex puzzle or taking action. It is not only about vibrant action and courage. Nor is leadership simply is a matter of dynamic presence and self-assured ambiance. And leadership is not solely an affair of the heart—linking with people on an emotional basis or acting out of emotional commitment. It is not only about connecting with people in tight relationships. Actually it is about all of these things together, all at one time, every moment. Leadership is complex only in that it has to come authentically from the entire being of the person. Brains are not enough. Good intentions are not enough. Goodwill is not enough. Processes are not enough.

Leadership involves intellect, heart, soul, and spirit. Leaders who do not understand who they are in for short tenures, extreme anxiety, or nagging frustration in not meeting what they want to accomplish. We have a total sense of identity—not simply the "part" of me that is a leader.

In addition, leadership is about what is trying to emerge. Joseph Jaworski believes that leadership is the capacity to collectively sense what is trying to emerge and bring it forth as it desires. He believes that we must have a sense of oneness and help collapse the boundaries that block cohesion and connectedness and shield what is trying to emerge or self-organize. We have to eliminate the blind spots that stop us from seeing the natural world, the oneness of humanity, and the power of intentions and collective thought.

Figure 8.1 defines the total "being" of leadership. Leadership involves the head, heart, and spirit. Leaders do not work in isolation but in relationship. The first relationship necessary is with themselves if they are to have quality relationships with others.

Most leaders and organizations focus on the head and ignore the heart and spirit of leadership. Leaders "know" in a variety of ways if they are in tune with the universe. Certainly we learn cognitively. The skills of analysis, synthesis, and evaluation are important, as are comprehension and understanding. But simply being smart is not enough. The main thesis of the book *The Best and the Brightest* is that the best minds can get us into quagmires and extreme difficulty because being smart and having analytical data are not sufficient.[14] Compassion, empathy, intuition, and moral "sense" are also required.

Leaders also need a "feel"—those street smarts and intuitive insights that can create greater understanding of events and activities because of an intangible "sense." Feel is one of these "soft" virtues that good leaders and athletes have. Some believe that you cannot teach feel, but you can teach analysis and evaluation, which are process driven. Many smart people fall short on "feel" even though they are bright and good thinkers.

Feel is related to intuition. We learn in many ways, not simply through our cognitive processes. Intuition involves the heart and spirit because even when we do not have facts, knowledge, logic, or reasoning we get an intuitive sense of the right and wrong of what to do.

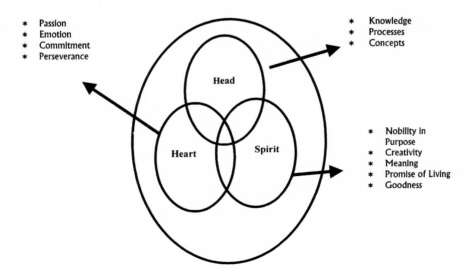

Figure 8.1. Leadership and Being

Intuition is knowing your job in a deeper sense than simply understanding or analyzing numbers and processes. It involves the subtleties and intangibles of energy, feelings, and fields.

Leaders need all of these attributes to be successful. Peter Senge indicates:

> People with high levels of personal mastery do not set out to integrate reason and intuition. Rather, they achieve it naturally—as a byproduct of their commitments to use all the resources at their disposal. They cannot afford to choose between reason and intuition, or head or heart, any more than they would choose to walk on one leg or see with one eye.[15]

The world is not always a rational place, and we certainly need our heads to try to understand what we can of its operation. But we also have a duty to create new knowledge and develop concepts to better understand the concrete and abstract aspects of our environment and reality. We can even better understand the chaotic nature of the systems in which we live and the disequilibrium that flows around us. Our heads—the logical and cognitive potential we have—allow us to do that and to formulate processes and practices to address circumstances.

Leaders need to be smart and be able to use the skills of analysis, synthesis, and evaluation that can lead to better problem solving. Our minds are a very important part of us, but we are not our minds alone—there is more to us that is important in leading.

In speaking of great leaders, heart is always mentioned because it drives focus and commitment. Leaders are passionate and have a deep commitment to serve. Emotions are always a part of life in our families and organizations, and leaders who lack emotion generally cannot connect with the common person. Emotions cover the gamut—from joy to anger. We cannot do our work unless we love it, we cannot help people without compassion, and we cannot right wrongs without indignation.

Heart also has to do with the intangible of courage because sometimes we must move from our comfort to the edge of pain. The pain can be mental anguish, emotional discomfort, or even the physical exhaustion it takes to do what is right. Our heart directs us to do what is right in the face of great odds or jeopardy and it commits us to others and to great causes. Our hearts cause us to see compassionately and to lead by outrage when injustice and tyranny are present.

Finally, inside of all of us lives the human spirit. People want spirited leadership that is creative, imaginative, inspired, resourceful, and innovative. Spirit, however, also speaks to goodness, promise, and meaning. As bundles of potential, born with free will and the ability to choose our own way, we are inquisitive and need to learn. Our spirit requires us to be open to what is new and also to let go of things we know in order to pursue virtue in life.

The spirit within us calls us to honorable causes and impels us to do something good and meaningful with our lives. To live a life of purpose and promise as a human in being is the key to personal fulfillment and happiness.

In looking at leadership as part our being, we must remember the following:

- Leaders touch the heart and spirit, as well as the mind. Commitment comes from the heart and through connection with other people.
- Leaders understand the tangible and intangible forces at work in organizations. That is why relationships are primary, connections are critical, and an awareness of invisible fields is required.
- Leaders recognize that collective thinking is a very powerful force that can help things emerge. Creativity, imagination, productivity, and commitment will surface only if we penetrate the barriers and defenses between people. We must eliminate the blind spots that stop what wants to emerge in our relationships and our world.
- Leaders see the world as an integral place of disequilibrium, chaos, and nonrationality that is also self-organizing, harmonious, and self-renewing. This world, however, is orderly because the force of values and principles can get us through confusion with integrity.
- Leaders take the risk of being their true selves and not acting as aloof loners who are above the fray. They are passionate about ideas and principles and delight in humanity and its potential. They express values and live up to them and have integrity of purpose and process. They are honest and genuine in working with others.

Rilke, in his poem "Just as the Winged Energy of Delight," indicates that the gods themselves learn from our doing the work we do.

> Just as the winged energy of delight
> carried you over many chasms early on,
> now raise the daringly imagined arch
> holding up the astounding bridges.
>
> Miracle does not lie only in the amazing
> living through and defeat of danger;
> miracles become miracles in the clear
> achievement that is earned.
>
> To work with things is not hubris
> when building the association beyond words;
> denser and denser the pattern becomes—
> being carried along is not enough.

Take your well-disciplined strengths
and stretch them between two
 opposing poles. Because inside human beings
is where God learns.[16]

Leadership is a calling, not a job. It is our work in the best sense of the word; the work we are supposed to do as a part of our whole being. It is not about power, it is about moral purpose.

CALLING

Our mythology says that leaders "answer the call." But what is the call? A calling is more complicated than responding to day-to-day issues. Calling and leading a meaningful life are inextricably entangled. The reason for our "being" is to find purpose and significance in life through pursuing our calling. People want to do something meaningful in life that has a positive impact on their families and communities. They do not want to live insignificant, meaningless lives. It takes courage to make ourselves known to the world in all our uniqueness.

Our drives can lead us to not being who we want or are destined to be. Destiny does not always wait if we do not have the courage to examine our lives and our state of being in order to take the first steps to reach our calling and destiny. These drives are connected to our attachments.

Gandhi believed that leaders must understand their attachments; otherwise those attachments, such as power, privilege, and possessions, can be corrupting influences. For example, our need for security may compromise our ability to speak out on controversial issues. Attachments can develop into drives that can destroy leaders. These drives include:

- *Guilt*: Some of us are manipulated by memories of past failures. While we are products of the past, we should not be prisoners of it.
- *Resentment and Anger*: Leadership is not easy, and it comes with bumps and failures, some which are by the design of others. Not letting go of these hurts and wounds can lead to acting out of anger and resentment, which only breeds more of the same. Getting even, 'clamming up," and blowing up are destructive. Practicing forgiveness and letting go is the only constructive way to address these situations.
- *Fear*: Leaders are attached to competence, and hence they may fear taking risks that are essential to success. Fear is a self-imposed prison that constrains our creativity and causes us to avoid risk and avoid traumatic and unpleasant experiences. Leadership is not a matter of playing it safe.

- *Materialism*: Being driven by materialism can deter leaders from doing what should be done. It can corrupt their efforts if they use their position for individual gain.
- *Need for Approval*: We all want approval and love. But at what cost? We can lose ourselves in the pursuit of approval from others. This approval is hollow because the lives of others is to be lived by them—they only get one life, not ours, too. Having others' expectations dominate our lives can be a joyless existence, one that will haunt us as we move through life and into old age.

Pursuing drives can create problems, even if the things people want you to do are laudable. Parker Palmer says, "When I follow only oughts, I find myself doing work that is ethically laudable but not mine to do. A vocation that is not mine, no matter how externally valued, does violence to self. . . . It violates my identity and integrity. When I violate myself, I invariably end up violating the people I work with."[17] We must use our gifts in a way significant to us. To do otherwise, regardless of how noble the effort, will be hollow. Inside of us is a drive to be what we are here for; our journey is unique. Our calling is not always easy to find. Adolescents sometimes call out in frustration, "I wish someone would just tell me what I am to do with my life." But Herman Hesse writes, "Each person has only one vocation—to find the way himself. His task is to discover his known destiny—not an arbitrary one—and live it wholly and resolutely within himself."[18]

We would like guarantees that in pursuit of our destiny everything will turn out all right. We want an airbag that will protect us from the crashes and hurts of living. James Hillman, the noted psychologist, believes we all have a destiny according to myth. We each are given "a unique daemon before we are born, and it has selected an image or pattern we live on earth. This soul-companion, the daemon, guides us here"[19] and is the carrier of our destiny. Life has risks, and the journey from beginning to end can be wonderful. Diane Ackerman says it in a brilliant way:

> The great affair, the love affair with life, is to live as variously as possible, to groom one's curiosity like a high-spirited thoroughbred, climb aboard, and gallop over the thick, sun-struck hills every day. Where there is no risk, the emotional terrain is flat and unyielding, and, despite all its dimensions, valleys, pinnacles, and detours, life will seem to have none of its magnificent geography, only a length. It began in mystery, and it will end in mystery, but what a savage and beautiful country lies in between.[20]

To live life in this way or to lead people takes optimism in the throes of the tragic and difficult circumstances we experience. Viktor Frankl believed that optimism is essential throughout life because it can turn suffering into human achievement and accomplishment and can help us turn guilt into opportunity to change ourselves for the better.[21] Optimism requires us to take action. Pessimists and cynics throw up their arms and curse the darkness. Optimists do not, and leaders show people another way in difficult times that is motivating and ennobling. Transformational leaders reach for the highest ideals that can change attitudes and behavior. Cynics cannot be transformational leaders as a matter of definition.

Always be a first-rate version of yourself, instead of a second-rate version of somebody else.

—Judy Garland

Our calling really boils down to things that are simply said but not always easily lived. Calling requires us to speak the truth, live with integrity to our gifts and ourselves, and reach a sense of wholeness, which results in a sense of happiness.

Frankl proposes that we should not pursue happiness but pursue a reason to be happy—our calling.[22] James MacGregor Burns, the noted historian, equates happiness with great values. Burns indicates that it can take several forms—he believes that happiness is a psychological or social feeling of fulfillment, of effectiveness, of relating to what is going on in the world, and of doing more than taking care of yourself. Happiness is finding our internal voice and developing a sense of efficacy, which can lead to happiness.[23]

Frankl, in his definitive work *Man's Search for Meaning*, indicates that in the death camps the prisoner who lost faith in the future quickly perished. When people lose hope, they lose their spiritual hold on life. The poet Lisel Mueller, in the poem "Hope," says:

> It hovers in dark corners
> before the lights are turned on,
>   it shakes the sleep from its eyes
>   and drops from mushroom gills,
>   it explodes in the starry heads
>   of dandelions turned sages,
>   it sticks to the wings of green angels
>   that sail from the tops of maples.

It sprouts in each occluded eye
of the many-eyed potato,
   it lives in each earthworm segment
      surviving cruelty,
         it is the motion that runs
           from the muses to the tail of a dog,
              it is the mouth that inflates the lungs
                 of the child that has just been born.

It is the singular gift
we cannot destroy in ourselves,
the argument that refuses death,
the genius that invents the future,
all we know of God.

It is the serum which makes us swear
not to betray one another;
it is this poem, trying to speak.[24]

Hope is anchored in each of us, even in the darkest times. No matter how hard or brutal life is, we have a choice. We can choose our attitude in any situation. Being hopeful is not being a Pollyanna—it is choosing to see opportunity in each situation. It is the spiritual freedom that can make life meaningful and purposeful.

Frankl believes that we have a responsibility to find meaning in life; it does not just find us. The more we give ourselves to a cause and serve others, the more likely we are to actualize our gifts and ourselves. We can only detect the meaning of our lives if we take responsibility to find the answer to life's problems and challenges. Life is not about self-gratification and desires. We must find what has significance to us and satisfies our desire for meaning.

Sometimes we wish things would be calm and serene. Frankl believes that the struggle to achieve a worthwhile goal and the call of potential meaning are positive forces, even if they involve tension and disequilibrium. Bohm, the physicist, agrees with Frankl. "The crisis of meaning is not only a crisis of culture, it is also a crisis of consciousness, for meaning is at the core of consciousness."[25] He believes that significance, value, and purpose are parts of consciousness. Nothing has a high value if it does not have significance to us, and what has significance indicates our purpose. We cannot lead mechanical lives.

In a sense, in searching for meaning, we must ask the right questions. The question is not "What do we expect from life?" The question is "What does life expect of us?" What calls us?

NOTES

1. Heraclitus. www.forthnet.gr/presocratics, accessed March, 2005.

2. In ancient Chinese religious practices, dogs would be shaped out of straw for ritual offerings to the spirits. The straw dogs would be treated with deference and exaggerated respect prior to their ceremonial use. Once they served their purpose, they were discarded.

3. Whyte, David, "Loaves and Fishes," in *House of Belonging*. Langley, WA: Many Rivers, 2002, p. 88.

4. Hock, Dee. *Birth of the Chaordic Age*. San Francisco: Berrett-Koehler, 1999, p. 224.

5. Eckhart, Meister. www.thedailyinspiration.com, accessed August, 2004.

6. Bohm, David. *Wholeness and the Implicate Order*. New York: Routledge, 1980, p. 3.

7. Bohm, David, and Mark Edwards. *Changing Consciousness*. New York: HarperCollins, 1991, pp. 3–6.

8. Wheatley, Margaret. *Leadership and the New Science*. San Francisco: Berrett-Koehler, 1992, p. 24.

9. Palmer, Parker. *Let Your Life Speak*. San Francisco: Jossey-Bass, 2000, p. 79.

10. Gandhi. *The Words of Gandhi*. New York: Newmarket, 2000, p. 4.

11. Roosevelt, Theodore. www.brainyquote.com, accessed October, 2004.

12. Palmer, *Let Your Life Speak*, p. 71.

13. Szymborska, Wislawa. "Our Ancestors' Short Lives," in *View with a Grain of Sand*. New York: Harcourt Brace, 1993, p. 143.

14. Halberstam, David. *The Best and the Brightest*. New York: Ballantine, 1969.

15. Senge, Peter, quoted in Gay Hendricks and Kate Ludeman. *The Corporate Mystic*. New York: Bantam, 1996, p. 90.

16. Rilke, Rainer Maria. "Just as the Winged Energy of Delight," in *The Rag and Bone Shop of the Heart: A Poetry Anthology*, edited by Robert Bly. New York: HarperCollins, 1993.

17. Palmer, Parker. *The Courage to Teach*. San Francisco: Jossey-Bass, 1998, p. 30.

18. Hesse, Herman. *Demian: The Story of Emile Sinclair's Youth*. New York: Bantam, 1965, p. 108.

19. Hillman, James. *The Soul's Code*. New York: Random House, 1996, p. 8.

20. Ackerman, Diane. *A Natural History of the Senses*. New York: Vintage, 1991, p. 309.

21. Frankl, Viktor. *Man's Search for Meaning*. Ashland, OR: Blackstone Audiobooks, 1995.

22. Frankl, *Man's Search*.

23. Burns, James MacGregor. Interview, *Compass Magazine*, Center for Public Leadership.

24. Mueller, Lisel. *Alive Together: New and Selected Poems*. Baton Rouge: Louisiana State University Press, 1996.

25. Bohm and Edwards, *Changing Consciousness*, p. 203.

The Promise of Living

They cannot content themselves with the time-honored process of stuffing students like sausages or even the possibly more acceptable process of training them like seals. It is the obligation of the schools and colleges to instill in their students the attitudes toward growth, learning, and creativity that will in turn shape the society.

—John W. Gardner

Schools are about the promise of living. They are not about organizational structures, power, procedures, or management. They are about living, fully and completely, with the heart as well as the head, physically as well as intellectually, and intuitively as well as logically. Schools are not about materials, technology, or methods. They are about relationships and interactions that form the nucleus around which learning and growth occur. As people experience diverse relationships, they learn more and more about themselves. Children do not become educated without the energy created from a deep connection with teachers, peers, and others.

Yet the literature about schools gives you a different message. We have turned our schools into factories and complex organizations. We talk of power, metrics, decisions, authority, and participation, from top-down to bottom-up to both-ends-toward-the-middle. We agonize over the distribution of power and control. These are the games adults play. We are stuck in procedures and regulations and trapped in redesigning structures and policy. Schools have become enamored with systems, focused on management, and bloated with jargon. They have become cold, impersonal, and competitive places concerned with test scores at a time when children need warm, caring, and nurturing environments. We are *re*engineering, *re*structuring, or *re*programming schools as if children were not a part of them. In the process, we have forgotten the nature of childhood development, complete with its joys and travails.

Instead, we should be giving thanks for our children. They all come to school with hope and love. They are full of anticipation and joy about learning and growing into adults. The curiosity and magic of a kindergarten classroom is testament to the natural excitement and energy children bring to school. It's natural, it's innocent, and it's genuine. Fostering and building on those qualities, not destroying them through impersonal, mechanistic, and factory-like environments, make schools special places that celebrate the unique destiny each child brings to this world.

Schools ought to be places where people have their heads in the clouds, not buried in systems or policy manuals. Ideals drive schools, not procedures or regulations. Ideals are hard to define and reach because they float high in the sky beyond our fingertips, but always offering the allure of greatness. The pragmatists, on the other hand, wring the idealism and the spontaneity out of schools. They want everything spelled out, all contingencies covered, and instantaneous measurable results. Schools are not about trivial, pragmatic outcomes: they must pursue profound and noble goals. They are serious places of learning with excitement and creativity, and of the successes and failures that come with striving. Great teachers fuse poetry with purpose and imagination with reality. To get imaginative schools, we need to change how we perceive schools.

The best metaphor for school is that of a sanctuary. The term *sanctuary* has a spiritual derivation. In ancient times, sanctuaries were the most sacred part of temples and were consecrated places that offered inviolable asylum, shelter, and refuge. Children need schools that offer them the sanctity to be themselves, to learn and grow, and to take risks so they can gather the experience of life without paying devastating prices. In these "sanctuaries" human genius in all it forms is honored, and the efforts of children who persevere with intensity, drive, and integrity of purpose are applauded.

Schools as sanctuaries are not cold, impersonal, tomblike places. They have a deep sense of soul, a passionate spirit, and strong emotional bonds and intellectual challenges. These educational sanctuaries encompass the following qualities:

- *Wonder*-ful—The inexplicable wonder of learning is in the air because the imagination and creativity of children are not lost. Curiosity is more than a spelling word. Children are spontaneous and like to explore and ask offbeat questions or make the unusual comment that spurs more thought and reflection. Children and adults delight in creative perception and unique syntheses of ideas. The expressiveness of childhood is not lost as children share their views of the world and learn new things. We all learn through sharing stories and passing on traditions and cere- monies, and we grow through experience and exploration. Innocence, with its reluctance to accept the conventional, is the catalyst that pro- duces the magic of learning in its purist form.

- *Reverent*—Wisdom is revered and all children have the opportunity to gain information and knowledge and see how both the head and the heart are important in life. Regardless of their ability or station in life, children learn their responsibilities and obligations and experience those things that would be unimaginable without the guidance and affectionate prod- ding of teachers or mentors. Education is valued because it liberates the mind and the spirit by helping students break self-imposed limitations and cultivates the boundless potential of their lives.

  Children's learning is important work and needs to be perceived that way by everyone in schools. That work is to be cherished, for it comes from the minds of children and is evidence of their developing spirit and destiny. Too frequently we think the work of children is less valuable than that of adults. In some schools, children's work is interrupted, ig- nored, or trivialized—when, in fact, it is as important to children as what their parents produce on their jobs. Work is to be revered because it is the expression of the human spirit.

- *Passionate*—Schools, as sanctuaries, are not places of ambivalence and neutrality. They abound with passion, just like the children within them. Educating children invokes strong, deep feelings of excitement and effi- cacy, transforming passion into commitment driving teachers and others to create joyful places of imagination and learning for children. People driven by passion cannot create anything less. Passion is the ground in which commitment and energy are anchored. Coupled with persever- ance, passion gives birth to the music of our imagination.

- *Connected*—In schools with a soul there is a feeling that children belong and are connected to the people within the school, as well as those in the outside world. These connections are important. As sanctuaries, schools are clear on their values and ideals; they build strong bonds with children and their families

  Children are not "customers" who have a fleeting interaction with the school based on mercenary motives like profit or ego. A number on a test or the length of their portfolio does not determine their value. They are more like family members who need long-term attention and care through unbreakable emotional bonds. These bonds allow children to feel safe to explore the outside world and see where and how they fit into it. In addition, children see the connections of knowledge and concepts between the disciplines, and recognize the similarities in how people think across disciplines. Children link thinking and feeling and become fully aware of all of their faculties and senses. They understand that the heart and the intellect are equally important, and they begin to see themselves as competent, complete people.

As children grow and move through the various stages of development, they require nurturing and support. Some are confident and others feel pressure to be accepted. At times children can feel like damaged goods as they make their way through life. David Whyte, in his poem "What to Remember When Waking," has a wonderful stanza about our relationship to the greater world and ourselves. He says,

> . . . You are not
> a troubled guest
> on this earth,
> you are not
> an accident
> amidst other accidents
> you were invited
> from another and greater
> night
> than the one
> from which
> you have just emerged.[1]

Children and adults have to remember that we are not mistakes, but instead are divine beings interconnected by our humanity and here on earth to contribute our unique gifts and purpose. Schools are not as much molders as they are nurturers of the talent and gifts we have within us. In this regard, there are no overachievers; if children perform, they had that ability inside of them, sometimes buried in a corner of their heart and soul that standardized tests cannot detect or assess.

- *Focused on Purpose*—In these schools everyone is a learner—children and adults. They share the excitement of learning something new and of struggling with mastering new things. The curriculum reflects broad and strong philosophical and academic understandings in all the disciplines.

Children also gain an understanding of the difficult problems with which human beings must wrestle, and realize that creating solutions to them takes a heart with its entire range of emotions and feelings, as well as brainpower. Too frequently children get the idea that heads are more important than hearts because schools are so driven by cognitive goals and standards. Schools as sanctuaries cherish the intellect *and* celebrate matters of the heart and spirit. They nurture character and goodness, as well as knowledge and skills.

- *Idealistic*—Strong ideals that are very difficult, if not impossible, to reach exemplify schools that are sanctuaries. Because the ideals are lofty and decent, people in the school become better simply by striving to reach them. Excellence comes from the stretch to reach the unattainable and to question what is. There is no settling for the pedestrian goals of basic literacy or application skills. Sanctuaries pursue virtue, justice, beauty, equality, goodness, liberty, and democracy. These schools discuss these issues and teach students about them so they can gain the wisdom to act on them.

- *Safe*—Children have a right to feel safe physically, emotionally, and intellectually. Safety of the mind and spirit, as well as body, needs to be a part of every school. In today's world safety is viewed narrowly in terms of physical violence. But children need protection from verbal assaults, emotional muggings, and intellectual attacks. They need the warmth of compassion to express feelings and emotions, the security to express ideas no matter how divergent or imaginative, and the assurance that they do not have to worry about their physical safety. Adults are careful with children, respecting them as people, and providing care and nurturing for all students. In safe schools, there are no haves and have-nots, chosen ones and outcasts. There is no mold all children must fit. All children are safe to be who they are, as products of their heritage, parents, potential, and experience.

OF IDEALS, IMAGINATION, AND COURAGE

As sanctuaries, schools are special places, because in them hearts, spirits, and intellects are tightly coupled. Children learn what's important in life and what isn't. Getting a job is important, but it isn't the sole reason children need an education. Children need to follow what calls to them from deep in their spirit and soul. The curriculum is based on issues all of us—children and adults—face in life. Our children need to consider the great questions of justice, liberty, equity, beauty, virtue, truth, and goodness. All of the disciplines, in one way or another, address one or more of them. Aren't they the issues around which we build our public lives? Aren't our personal relationships and interests wrapped up in these issues? Don't academics, fine arts, trades, technology, and extracurricular activities revolve around them in one form or another?

Too frequently, though, we really do not believe that students can come to grips with important philosophical issues. So we package programs in an array of practical experiences or rote worksheets, as if pragmatism were all that mattered in life. But reality requires that children gain wisdom about abstract issues like liberty and justice so they can have an intellectual and moral structure to cope with the practicalities of life. Children can master knowledge, skills, understanding, and wisdom in academics and other areas if they are given the chance to think with their heads and to feel with their hearts. Searching for truth is a factor of the heart working with the head, rather than the brain functioning alone.

Sanctuaries allow for imagination. Children's imagination is a mark of genius and humanness. Seeing opportunities in dark times is a factor of imagination. Having the ability to confront and deal with problems resourcefully is a part of imagination. Cooperating or competing requires inspiration and creativity. Imagination creates vision that is fresh, inspired, and poetic. It moves beyond the expected and conventional into a whole new way of perceiving and understanding.

To be imaginative in school or the world requires courage. Courage is a matter of heart. Pushing against the grain, standing up for principles, and holding one's own against peers, conventional wisdom, and "the way we always do things" takes strength of character. There are many smart people with comprehensive knowledge and skills who do nothing when confronted with adversity or cruelty. They may be afraid of consequences or lack confidence.

Children must learn that there are many heroes in life, not just those spotlighted on television and in movies. Heroism is more than physical exploits; many times courage is about standing on principles and ideas. Heroes are individuals just like themselves who act on strong feelings and a high spirit that is an outgrowth of conviction. They have the mental strength to persevere and withstand pressure because they have moral confidence that encourages and sustains them and others. Bravery is necessary for everyone to survive in life at one time or another. It is certainly a pragmatic requirement at work and in the world. Imagination and courage are encouraged and appreciated, along with the cultivation of content, skills, and knowledge.

> When your children see you choose, without hesitation, without remark, to value virtue more than security, to love more than you fear, they will learn what courage looks like and what love serves, and they will dread its absence.
>
> —John McCain, U.S. senator

We must jettison the old view of schools as bureaucratic organizations that should run like businesses and look at the "bottom line" of profit margin. These places often put adults' learning over children's and see themselves as "molders" of children's lives, places where competition and material success are fundamental. These schools are prevalent because of society's short-term strategy of trying to find a "cure" for schools based on the needs of businesses and the marketplace.

We must also abandon the fear of failure. We fear not measuring up and quake in the face of change and its impact on us. Fear drives out compassion, and it destroys creativity and initiative. It saps our emotional and intuitive resources, and causes us to rely on measurable and "scientific" solutions that stand the test of linear logic. Most people still have a very fragmented view of education and life itself. We value linear science to the point that we cannot see the complex and integral whole that constitutes what being educated means—and what being human is.

People today are searching for a sense of connection to one another, to their community, and to something larger than themselves. They need purpose to drive out the encroaching hollowness that contemporary life can create. That hollowness of diversion, trivial pursuits, and cynicism can be thwarted only by a sense of one's soul and by viewing the world through the emotional and moral portals of ones' heart—*and* through the lens of cognitive logic. In our hearts we all want to trust in the invisible, abstract forces of virtue and goodness. These magnets of the head and heart can attract new ideas, commitment, and imagination.

In schools with a sense of their soul and virtue, educators and parents create sanctuaries that have the whole child as the center of the experience. They develop a sense of community around educating children, and they develop an ongoing dialogue about the discrepancy between "what is" and "what can be." The focal point is long-term care for the children. In these environments, children are appreciated for their uniqueness. There is an unwavering commitment to respecting all children and the talents they possess, and to ensuring the success and development of each.

In sanctuaries the Second World of the inner self takes precedence, so that at the end of their formal education each child feels a sense of wholeness of head and heart, and grasps the meaning of happiness. Children are not molded, but instead are allowed to find themselves through the interactions they have with people, ideas, and experiences.

Finally, in order to fulfill the promise of living, schools must have a spirit of loyalty and courage. We must be loyal to the wonderment of childhood in all its stages. We must examine it and nourish it and value it as deeply as we cherish adulthood. We must look through the eyes of a child and focus the lens of reform so that change will improve the quality of life for all children. To do so takes courage, because open discussion of schools as sanctuaries and matters of the heart brings scoffing and charges of naïveté from those whose perception is stuck in the quicksand of engineering and pragmatism. To be an idealist takes courage, and to champion the cause of educating children in matters of the intellect and the heart takes true heroism.

NOTE

1. Whyte, David. *House of Belonging*. Langley, WA: Many Rivers Press, 1997, p. 27.

Epilogue: The Essence of Leadership

Wisdom is about living harmoniously in the universe, which is itself a place of order and justice that triumphs over chaos and employs chance for its ultimate purpose.

—Matthew Fox

The preceding chapters have used poetry and other images to help focus on leadership in a different way: a way that tries to touch the very humanity that makes a difference in leaders, in the way we work, and in how we can make a lasting contribution with our lives.

As I have said many times, leadership is not about procedures or data; it is about people's hopes and dreams—their aspirations to reach the potential that lies within them. Leadership is important if it calls people to reach for the noble, for the good, and for the wholeness that connects us all. Sometimes our science, in an effort to understand the universe, uses a plane of thought that fragments and causes us, to use the old cliché, to miss the forest for the trees.

In that sense, poets see the integral nature of our inner and outer lives, they see the connections between people and their aspirations, they see connections between people and their relationships, they see connections between dreams and reality and between ideals and creativity. They see how interconnected we are physically, emotionally, cognitively, and spiritually. They see that while logical and linear science can help us understand the world, cold statistics and rational processes do not make a life or address the integral nature of the world. They also understand that control does not rest in our hands; that sometimes bigger and unseen forces affect our lives.

Leaders are like gardeners who plant seeds, nourish the soil, love and respect the natural order of things, and work in fields where life happens with its joy and pain. They are not engineers who can control all processes and duplicate things repetitively with precision. Thank God for that. People do not respond in prescribed ways because they come with their own personalities, histories, and longings. There are no duplicate people. Processes and data do not motivate people the way ideas, emotions, and principles do. The "whys" of life speak louder to us than the "hows" of living and doing things.

As we grow older, we learn that life is fleeting—it hangs on a narrow, gossamer thread of fate. In the time we have, we have to make something of our lives that moves beyond our own self-interest. In *Saving Private Ryan*, as the captain lay on the bridge dying, he said to Private Ryan "Earn this. Earn it,"[1] as Ryan faced living the rest of his life. How we "earn this" life is at the core of leadership.

In the book *Presence*, Senge, Sharmer, Jaworski, and Flowers address the soft issues of leadership. They argue against the fragmentation of thought and organizations and the obsession with data and measurability. Reality is not always anchored in seeing and measuring things. Many managers believe that only what is measured is heeded, that concrete goals outdistance "soft" ones. But what is the measure of a life—of our lives?

The authors state:

> Not only does overreliance on measurement doom modern society to continuing to see a world of things rather than relationships, it also gives rise to the familiar dichotomy of the "hard stuff" [what can be measured] versus the "soft stuff" [what can't be measured]. If what's measurable is "more real," it's easy to relegate the soft stuff, such as the quality of interpersonal relationships and people's sense of purpose in their work, to a secondary status. This is ironic because the soft stuff is often the hardest to do well and the primary determinant of success or failure. For example, engineers know that the best technical solutions often fail to be implemented, or are not successful when they are, because of low trust and failed communication.[2]

We should not fall into the habit of polarized thinking: that one thing is good and the other is bad. We have had enough of that in education and politics. There is a place for measurement as long as it doesn't restrict us to pedestrian and mediocre aspirations. The problem is when we cannot differentiate between the importance of what can be measured and what cannot. A problem exists when we get out of balance and become so dependent on measurable data that it eliminates judgment, intuition, and learning. When data "drives" leaders to push people, and manage by fear, it becomes counterproductive and harmful to success and to people.

As Senge and coauthors state, "it's not possible to measure a relationship."[3] Leadership is all about relationships, because organizations are webs of interrelated relationships. To apply strictly quantitative measures to qualitative endeavors like leadership, learning, and commitment is to build on a false premise—essentially that reality is what you can measure and that you can engineer excellence into schools and organizations.

While we yearn for the certainty in measurable data, leaders live on a different plane and are subservient to a different master. Over the centuries and in many traditions, leaders and wisdom have been indelibly connected. We want wise leadership that embodies the truth and knowledge of the past, the sacred values of life, and the essential principles of justice, liberty, and goodness.

Today, it seems, we seldom speak of wisdom, leadership, and character. But we do speak of leadership and cleverness. Of manipulation. Of winning. Of ego. Of control. The news and the media are full of those images as people posture and strut.

Wisdom, according to James Hillman, is about knowledge, soul, life, death, initiation, and values.[4] The Greek word *sophia* comes from the crafts—carpentry and handwork. Wise people are "tillers" who make small adjustments and move to keep the "boat" of life on course in changing winds. Wisdom is shown in our chiseled faces by the adjustments we made to confront gentle winds and the dark, painful storms in life's journey.

Wisdom and the pursuit of truth are part of that journey. Leaders must be dedicated to the truth—in all its forms. But what does that mean? M. Scott Peck indicates that a life dedicated to truth is one of "continuous and never-ending stringent self-examination. We know the world through our relationship to it. . . . The life of wisdom must be a life of contemplation combined with action."[5]

In examining our lives, we must find own truth and wisdom. In an interview, Senge states that in the industrial era we developed a notion of truth as being "scientific truth" about the physical and manifest world. He indicates that there is an older definition of truth, which is the "truth of one's own experience as experienced." The problem, he says, is that experience cannot be reduced to a measurable concept or calibrated with any accuracy.[6]

Experience—the truth and wisdom of our own lives—comes from the "tilling" we do in adjusting to life's unfolding. This truth is valid in our relationships, as is the truth of statistical charts. Wisdom, nourished by values and principles, cannot be condensed into a mathematical formula.

In summary, leadership is about:

- new horizons, not benchmarks;
- character and wisdom, not scientific management;
- people, love, and commitment, not metrics.

CAUTIONS FOR LEADERS

Pressure and turmoil are a part of leadership. We experience an inward pressure to reach our own potential and to meet the challenges we face. Outward pressure also places great demands. Time pushes us to meet deadlines or to fulfill others' expectations "on time." The pace we set is frequently artificial and based on needs that have nothing to do with our purpose or success. The demand to produce an optimum result and be able to show it tangibly puts great weight on our shoulders.

Pressure can cause leaders to succumb to the allure of the sirens of quick fixes, gimmicks, or manipulation. Finding the single key—the ultimate answer—becomes a paramount goal. The problem is there isn't a single key.

Leaders understand that great virtues can become our biggest vices. In fact, many ethical dilemmas are not over matters of right or wrong principles. They are the offspring of right versus right principles—the intersection where two positive principles collide. For example, truth can collide with stewardship, equity bumps into equality, and fairness runs into consistency. Virtues raise difficult and uncomfortable questions and spur conflict. Unless we understand the downsides and dysfunctions of things, we cannot really apply them appropriately. In fact, when it comes to leadership, exploring the conflict between right and right principles can lead to creative and inspirational places for people to apply their talents.

Questioning the veracity of some things can make one look like a heretic. But leaders are supposed to raise questions. Accepting things glibly, without understanding, can turn promising ideas and approaches into disasters. We also have to be cautious of the following:

- *Metrics and Measurable Data*: Throughout this book, the concern is raised about our heavy and almost solitary reliance on metrics and data. The assumption is that if it is not measurable it is not important, or worse—if it's not measurable it does not exist and is not "real." Data-based decision making has a place, but that place should not be at the expense of those things that nurture creativity, imagination, and commitment. Data can inform decisions, but data are not always true reflections of what is. Emotion. Heart. Connection. Loyalty. Justice. All are important—and not easily measured. All people search for a sense of belonging in the world. There is no metric for that. And sometimes doing the right thing goes against the grain of data. Creativity is needed in life and schools, yet it cannot be seen, except as a result of human endeavor. As Goethe states: "Whatever you think you can do, or believe you can do, begin it, because action has magic, grace, and power."[7]

• *Technology*: No one can deny that technology is a great influence on society and a powerful force. The cliché "Technology is a great tool" is heard in almost every field—with poetry and spiritual practice the exceptions. The potential for efficiencies is great, but the penchant to think that technology is the ultimate answer is overblown. Schools are the best example, as research has shown little, if any, improvement in achievement through technology. In fact, technology has negative effects and dysfunctions—tools can also hurt people.

Technology is touted as bringing people together—connecting them digitally and electronically. That may be true at a superficial level. Connections, however, are more than mere ability to e-mail or talk to people over a device. Feeling a person's energy, looking into his or her eyes, or intuitively sensing the person's demeanor cannot be done through a computer screen, a cell phone, or a video monitor. These devices are immune to the subtlety of personality or the pain that rests in people's eyes and hearts. Individuals can digitally transmit data but not feelings or emotion, which require a medium more sensitive than a keyboard or camera.

In addition, technology is impersonal. Would you rather receive an e-mail or a handwritten note? E-mail is quick—its speed cannot be rivaled. E-mails, however, lack the soul and personality that our handwriting portrays. The art of letter writing is fading in the face of technology. There is more to a message than content. Handwritten letters are expressions of a person's total being—our script is unique to us, reflecting our personality; our sentences and paragraphs are devoid of the lexicon of e-mail shorthand; and the precious time it takes to write a letter also communicates and adds to the message. We can feel the person in the paper and sense their tenor in their writing, and even smell their perfume or aftershave. Our hearts and souls are more easily transmitted through the pen than the keyboard, just as seeing a person in the flesh is better than a photograph. Insipid recorded telephone menus frustrate people in the name of efficiency, when all people want is to connection with a human being.

Technology is fast—that is a virtue and a vice. The pace of our lives has increased and our patience has decreased because of instantaneous communication with and access to people. Speed can kill. And that goes for technology. It has helped to kill civility and reflection. People expect instant responses, and when they do not get them, they get angry. Our patience wears thin, and manners die. We hear conversations that are personal or we are privy to business dealings in restaurants, airports, airplanes, stores, and almost everywhere that cell phone service is available. They intrude on our privacy, solitude, and silence. This is no small thing in today's driven and frenzied society.

Technology also causes reflection and thought to dissolve in the rush for a quick response. Lawyers get proposals at 10:00 A.M. and are expected to meet with their clients and respond by 2:00 P.M. The emotions of clients are ignored or inflamed as people lose time to think and contemplate. Sometimes, a quick response creates greater difficulty than one that allows for emotions to cool and for people to thoroughly think through the issues. Finding silence and stillness is difficult in the age of technological immediacy. Reflection and the insight it brings are casualties.

The avalanche of data technology can manufacture also can stymie decision making or bury us under mountains of numbers, not all of which are of equal weight and importance. Important data can be obscured in the flurry, or the totality of the data can be insignificant and marginal. The idea that if it is charted and graphed, then it must be important is a dysfunction that can be perilous. Well-packaged data can look more important than they really are. Style in this case can supercede substance.

Data, must be turned into information, which "in-forms" decisions. We sometimes forget that unless we make sense of data, it becomes inconsequential. Analyzing and interpreting data with integrity and creating information and linking it with other ways of knowing—experience and intuition—are essential for good decisions.

Technology certainly appeals to our senses. Watch children viewing television—the swooshing sound effects, the visuals, the colors, the tone of voice, the movement, the total appeal catches their eyes and ears. The same is true of adults—observe what happens when a television is turned on in a room. Look at our newscasts—complete with music and sound effects and flashing headlines constantly scrolling in multiple tiers. Fred Rogers, a.k.a. Mr. Rogers, purposely went against the grain in children's television; his show was quiet and intimate, rather than boisterous, loud, and visually stimulating. He understood child development—children need quiet and personal attention and nurturing. So do we.

We can lose meaning amid all of the technological bombast. We can lose silence and reflection. We can lose what makes sense because technology offers stimulating and immediate responses to complex and serious questions. Blogs are not dialogues. The issue is how we can use technology intelligently and ensure that the meaning of what we do is not lost, that we don't create a raucous environment, and that ultimately technology doesn't matter more than people.

- *Business Systems*: There are things schools can learn from business—approaches to planning, entrepreneurial ideas, developing creative organizations, and management techniques. But—and it is a big but— schools are not businesses. Children are not customers. Schools are something different. There is a reverence about them that does not exist in any other institution in our society except spiritual ones. Schools are about care and nurturing, learning and growth, development and time, mistakes and wisdom.

In that vein, applying highly regulated, consistent, and uniform business practices is not always appropriate. Complexity is rampant in businesses and corporate life. Driven by the bottom line and cost-effectiveness, we have constructed large, impersonal schools where children get lost in the shuffle. Most businesses in towns are much smaller than the school systems and schools within them. Public school achievement is compared to that of private schools, most of which are far smaller and have a selective student body than their public school counterparts.

Schools have a sense of soul, which is about our sense of belonging. Children must feel that sense of belonging—a sense of participation, surprise, color, and intrigue. Without that sense of soul, schools become factories or warehouses. Wisdom and learning about values and life do not come out of a bottle, nor do they come at a specific time. Business can meet schedules and FedEx can help, but children's development emerges in its own time and in a manner that can only be nurtured by patience and love. Schools are sanctuaries.

- *Fear and Money*: People who are frightened and fearful cannot achieve their best. Maslow proved that with his need hierarchy. Yet many organizations run on fear and money—external efforts to control and motivate. Control systems based on fear produce self-inflicted wounds that can stymie success or kill the organization.

Scaring people into high performance has a limited impact over time, as does the influence of money—fiscal incentives—to drive people to higher levels of achievement. Fear and money can move people; they can't motivate them. Fear and money are like heroin—they can move people to do things, but as time goes by it takes greater measures, or more money, to move people the same distance as previously.

Leaders also fear being drawn to issues that they prefer not to face. Some of those issues come from inside the leader him- or herself. We can fear losing our identity if we fail in difficult circumstances. If our whole identity is wrapped up in our role, fear can deter leaders from taking a course of action that is dangerous and difficult. Fear pushes people to the safe shores of the comfort of the known.

WHAT CAN WORK

In a confounding world, we often look for complex answers. When chaos rings throughout the halls of the organization, we think that the answer must rest in multifaceted, complex systems. Because life is confusing, we think that the subtle and dynamic forces are immune to simpler approaches. That may not be the case.

In very simple terms, leaders need to connect to others on a real and personal basis—on a level that concerns ideals and values. Great leaders capture people's imagination and appeal to a sense of stewardship and to causes greater than people's own self-interest. Of course, there is no recipe or formula to accomplish this. Commitment cannot be engineered into the system. It must grow and be nurtured through approaches that have been at our disposal for centuries.

Sometimes we forget the power of those approaches, as our world seems to pick up speed and we sense globalization and increasing fragmentation and isolation. These paradoxes work against the efficacy people seek in their life's work and life. Instant communication, easy access to information, and great waves of technology are contrasted with the distance, hollowness, and emptiness many feel in their work and the lack of efficacy they sense in "empowered" environments.

Leaders can do several things that have been part of our society for years. First, conversation is important. Taking time for face-to-face conversation is a powerful force leaders can use to connect with people, provide a sense of clear purpose, build credibility, and learn new things. In conversation, people tell stories, and stories carry texture and nuance, feelings and morals. Author Clarissa Pinkola Estés, who wrote *Women Who Run with the Wolves*, writ stories present the knife of insight, the flame of the passionate life, the breath to speak what one knows, the courage to stand what one sees without looking away, the fragrance of the wild soul."[8]

Truth can be found in the wisdom modeled in stories. Experiential knowledge is something that professions should not ignore. Stories also put faces on issues and connect and bind people on levels beyond concepts and information.

A formal process to have conversation is the process of dialogue, in which we reach a deep and clear understanding of our values and of the reasons we think and feel the way we do. Masks drop, titles disappear, and human connection expands. Instead of debating or having superficial conversations, people risk sharing their ideas, values, and perceptions until a deep appreciation and understanding takes place that can lead to a common approach and commitment. Unfortunately, our desire for quick answers, bureaucratic distance between people, and ego-driven behavior can get in the way. Reflection and commitment can create collective thinking that can help cause new ideas to emerge or remove obstacles to what is naturally emerging.

In business we hear of the "bottom line" as strictly profit or cost-effectiveness. Using fiscal resources efficiently and effectively is important, but there are other bottom lines:

- *Quality Programs*: Offering excellent experiences and programs that achieve cognitive, psychomotor, and affective growth and fostering of human spirit are part of the bottom line for educators.
- *Melding Personal and Organizational Goals*: When people move toward "self-actualization" in their work, the organization is better because people are committed and motivated. Hiring highly competent and creative people demands that we help them fulfill themselves in the pursuit of their and our work—another important bottom line.
- *Relationships*: Organizations are living social systems with webs of relationships. Building positive interactions on trust, efficacy, commitment, and love is good for communication, loyalty, and the bottom line.
- *Success*: In all sectors of enterprise, the satisfaction of the people we serve is important to success. That means that nurturing, learning, and growth in all aspects of life—academic, ethics, principles, discipline, and relationships—is essential for students and adults.

An approach that can bring new perspectives and understanding is scenario planning, which was discussed earlier. What is already manifest is clear. What wants to emerge is something different, requiring using all of our senses and abilities. Intuition, emotion, brainpower, experience, data, and other forms of learning come to bear on determining plausible scenarios that organizations face. In addition, the ability to build in "future memory" by playing out the scenarios creates learning that can be applied to these situations should they arise. The power of thought (remember Bohm's theory of thought as system) can help positive scenarios emerge. Moving beyond strictly strategic planning, which is a linear extension of today, can help us brace for a future that can take an unusual course.

Looking at these scenarios, positive and negative, can help us grow. Nancy Wood, in her poem "Native Blessing," demonstrates the learning that can occur in difficult scenarios or circumstances.

> Bless these circumstances.
> Bless the hardship and the pain.
> Bless the hunger and the thirst.
> Bless the locusts and the drought.
> Bless the things that do not turn out right.
> Bless those who take all and give not.
> In these circumstances, find growth.
> In growth, find clarity.
> In clarity, an inner vision.[9]

Conversations, dialogue, scenario planning, and person-to-person contact can lead to this clarity. It cannot be done through e-mail, it cannot be done by keeping score. Aloof and distant leaders do not connect. Straightforward conversation and listening are two qualities that make leaders approachable and credible. Technology is impotent. Only people connected through a sense of belonging can bring about these changes and improve circumstances for children and themselves.

In addition, we can create contemplative organizations in which people find solitude and time to reflect. Being contemplative concerns being mindful and aware of the present moment; concentrating in a quiet, peaceful environment; and finding presence of mind. Self-control, balance, energy, zest, and pleasure can allow us to make sense of our challenges and actions.

LEADERSHIP: AN END NOTE

Leadership is truly a human and philosophical endeavor. It is not about things or systems, or processes and data. It is about people—you and me and who we are and what we can become together.

Life happens. It is serendipitous, exciting, painful, joyful, turbulent, quiet, harmonious, chaotic, and full of a broad array of twists and surprises that defy human expectation. All are immune to our meddling, except on the farthest insignificant fringes. We should celebrate life's textures and colors and deal with what is—in joyous as well as painful times, because we will not pass this way again, and our life can have great meaning to others—particularly our children.

John O'Donohue, the poet and author, writes, of looking at life: "Even though time will inscribe your face, weaken your limbs, make your movements slower, and, finally, empty your life, nevertheless there is still a place in your spirit that time never get near."[10]

Our spirit in leading a life that matters cannot be touched by the long fingers of time. Our spirit and character live beyond ourselves and can permeate people and the life of the organizations we lead.

We must be awake to what matters—tangible worldly assets do not make a life of great meaning or success. The old saying "Life is short" is all too true, because minutes and seconds pass with accelerating speed, and, before you know it, we are getting "younger toward death." But life is not a race. It is not about things. It is about consciously participating in it as authentically as we can.

Leaders who find their calling contribute to the commonweal and to help others fulfill themselves in noble pursuits. Spending time following great principles, tilting at windmills, can make a great difference in helping others see an inner vision of what can be.

> One word frees us of all the weight and pain of life: that would be love.
>
> —Sophocles

Knowing ourselves in the deepest way and understanding why we are here is the most difficult work we face; far more difficult and risky than reaching a bottom line, fulfilling a strategic goal, or showing tangible results. It is the biggest challenge that leaders need to confront in order to get the numbers they desire. Without that, the distance they communicate deafens the people they lead and buries the best plans and processes in the silt of ambivalence. Leadership is not about cleverness, deception, and winning. Cleverness may win the moment in the First World, but it will destroy the heritage and future of an organization and shatter the peace of the Second World.

So what can leaders do to help people use their full potential and reach for the stars against the odds? First, we can love what we do. We bring love into the context of leading because unless you love humanity you will not want to help people fulfill their potential and their calling. Leadership is not about ego and self. It is about humanity. Leaders love the people they lead—and they craft a tie that binds people together. They live in the Second World.

Leaders fashion an environment in which butterflies live—those small acts of butterfly wings flapping that create great currents of creativity and commitment, which make the world a better place to live and bring meaning to our existence on this planet. Leaders address our longing to belong by developing vessels in which our aspirations can be tied to those of others in a great effort that allows us to find nobility in our lives.

Leadership is about the pursuit of happiness. Pursuit means the ability to find our niche and help others—these things are not guaranteed. Happiness comes from finding our core as leaders, and living up to it in reaching for justice, liberty, equality, truth, beauty, and goodness in our lives, the lives of others, and most importantly, the lives of our children.

Vaclav Havel, the former leader of Czechoslovakia, said to the U.S. Congress that the "salvation of this human world lies nowhere else than in the human heart, in the human power to reflect, in human meekness and in human responsibility."[11] He wrote the poem "It Is I Who Must Begin" to address leaders' obligations:

> It is I who must begin.
> Once I begin, once I try—
> here and now,

right where I am,
not excusing myself
by saying that things
would be easier elsewhere,
without grand speeches and
ostentatious gestures,
but all the more persistently
—to live in harmony
with the "voice of Being," as I
understand it within myself
—as soon as I begin that,
I suddenly discover,
to my surprise, that
I am neither the only one,
nor the first,
nor the most important one
to have set out
upon that road.

Whether all is really lost
or not depends entirely on
whether or not I am lost.[12]

NOTES

1. *Saving Private Ryan.* A Steven Spielberg film, Dreamworks, November 1999.

2. Senge, Jaworski, Sharmer, Flowers. *Presence.* Society for Organizational Learning, 2004, p. 198.

3. Senge and Sharmer, *Presence*, p. 199.

4. Hillman, James. Interview, 1988, "Authenticity, Character, and Destiny."

5. Peck, M. Scott. *In Search of Stones.* New York: Hyperion, 1995.

6. Senge, Peter. Interview no. 15, by Otto Scharmer. Society of Learning Organizations.

7. Goethe. Quoted in Cameron, Julia. *Working in This World.* New York: Penguin-Putnam, 2002, p. 21.

8. Estés, Clarissa Pinkola. *Women Who Run with the Wolves.* New York: Ballantine, 1996, p. 19.

9. Wood, Nancy. "Native Blessing," in *Spirit Walker*, p. 67.

10. O'Donohue, John. *Eternal Echoes.* New York: Cliff Street Books, 1999, p. xxiii.

11. Havel, Vaclav. *The Art of the Impossible.* New York: Knopf, 1997, p. 18.

12. Havel, Vaclav. "It Is I Who Must Begin," in *Letter to Olga.* New York: Knopf, 1988.

Glossary

Authenticity: True to one's own personality, spirit, or character; fully trust-worthy as exactly what is claimed; unique.

Balance: Mental and emotional steadiness; inner peace; worldly and inner (spiritual) equilibrium; balance of modern and spiritual traditions.

Character: Moral excellence and firmness—essential nature; good thoughts; good conduct; rooted in principles.

Compassion: Sympathetic consciousness of another's plight with the desire to alleviate it; kindness; taking action to relieve suffering; engaging in service from the heart.

Courage: Mental or moral strength to venture, persevere, and withstand danger, fear, or difficulty; self-confidence; adhering to the truth; firm values.

Creativity: Inventiveness; bringing something new into existence; imaginative; search for meaning.

Dialogue: Exchange of ideas; speaking the truth; understanding deep values behind positions.

Empathy: Act of understanding, being aware and being sensitive to the thoughts, experiences, and expressions of others; the view that we are all fundamentally the same; sharing joys and sorrows.

Forgiveness: Giving up the resentment of or claim to requital, thereby allowing room for error or weakness; love for humanity; forbearance; seeing others as oneself.

Holistic Thinking: A complete systems focus—reflections, judgments, connections; sense of oneness; vision to see whole; conceptual thinking.

Inner Silence: Stillness; being near the center of your inner self; letting your mind rest; calmness; clearness.

Intuition: The power or faculty of attaining direct knowledge or cognition without evident, rational thought and inference; when your inner voice tells you what "is" and what "is not."

Reflection: Thinking calmly or quietly; peace; examination of spiritual/traditional truths.

Simplicity: Freedom from pretense; clarifying; reduction to basic elements; no exaggeration or falsification; sincere; straightforward.

Synthesis: The combining of often diverse conceptions into a coherent whole.

Trust: Assured reliability on the character, ability, strengths, and truth of someone; honor others.

Wisdom: The ability to discuss inner qualities and relationships; deep insight; not cleverness; seeing unity in diversity; seeing the integrated nature of the world; introspection from experience—pain and sorrow.

References

LEADERSHIP AND ORGANIZATIONS

Bohm, David (1994). *Thought as a system*. New York: Routledge.

—— (1996). *On dialogue*. New York: Routledge.

Burns, James MacGregor (1978). *Leadership*. New York: Harper Touchbooks.

—— (2003). *Transforming leadership*. New York: Atlantic Monthly Press.

Campbell, Joseph (1973). *The hero with a thousand faces*. Princeton, NJ: Princeton University Press.

Capra, Fritjof (1996). *The web of life: A new scientific understanding of living systems*. New York: Anchor.

Cashman, Kevin (1999). *Leadership from the inside out*. Provo, UT: Executive Excellence.

Crider, Tom (2000). *A nature lover's book of quotations*. Southbury, CT: Birch Tree.

Csikszentmihalyi, Mihaly (1990). *Flow: The psychology of optimal experience*. New York: Harper and Row.

—— (1996). *Creativity: Flow and the psychology of discovery and invention*. New York: Harper Collins.

de Geus, Arie (1997). *The living company*. Boston: Harvard Business School Press.

Fox, Matthew (2000). *Passion for creation: The earth-honoring spirituality of Meister Eckhart* (2nd ed.). Rochester, VT: Inner Traditions.

Fromm, Erich (2003). *On being human*. New York: Continuum International.

—— (2003). *To have or to be*. New York: Continuum International.

Gandhi, Mohandas (2000). *The words of Gandhi*. Edited by Richard Attenborough. New York: Newmarket.

Gardner, John W. (1990). *On leadership*. New York: Free Press.

George, Bill (2003). *Authentic leadership: Rediscovering the secrets to creating lasting value.* San Francisco: Jossey-Bass.

Gleick, James (1987). *Chaos.* New York: Penguin.

Goens, George A., and Sharon I. R. Clover (1987). *Getting the most from public schools: A parent's guide.* Englewood, FL: Pineapple Press.

—— (1991). *Mastering school reform.* Boston: Allyn and Bacon.

Hendricks, Gay, and Kate Ludeman (1996). *The corporate mystic: A guidebook for visionaries with their feet on the ground.* New York: Bantam Books.

Hillman, James (1996). *The soul's code: In search of character and calling.* New York: Random House.

—— (1999). *The force of character and the lasting life.* New York: Random House.

Hock, Dee (1999). *Birth of the chaordic age.* San Francisco: Berrett-Koehler.

Isaacs, William (1999). *Dialogue and the art of thinking together.* New York: Currency.

Jaworski, Joseph (1996). *Synchronicity: The inner path of leadership.* San Francisco: Berrett-Koehler.

Johnson, Steven (2001). *Emergence: The connected lives of ants, brains, cities, and software.* New York: Touchstone.

Moxley, Russ S. (2000). *Leadership and spirit: Breathing new vitality and energy into individuals and organizations.* San Francisco: Jossey-Bass.

Nair, Keshavan (1994). *A higher standard of leadership.* San Francisco: Berrett-Koehler.

Palmer, Parker J. (1998). *The courage to teach.* San Francisco: Jossey-Bass.

—— (2000). *Let your life speak.* San Francisco: Jossey-Bass.

Peck, M. Scott, M. D. (1995). *In search of stones: A pilgrimage of faith, reason, and discovery.* New York: Hyperion.

Ringland, Gill (1998). *Scenario planning: Managing for the future.* New York: John Wiley and Sons.

Schade, Edith Royce (1994). *From May Sarton's well: Writings of May Sarton.* Glastonbury, CT: Goodale Hill.

Schwartz, Peter (1991). *The art of the long view: Planning for the future in an uncertain world.* New York: Currency Doubleday.

Senge, Peter, C. Otto Scharmer, Joseph Jaworski, Betty Sue Flowers (2004). *Presence: Human purpose and the field of the future.* Cambridge, MA: Society for Organizational Learning.

Wheatley, Margaret J. (1992). *Leadership and the new science: Learning about organization from an orderly universe.* San Francisco: Berrett-Koehler.

—— (1999). *Leadership and the new science* (2nd ed.). San Francisco: Berrett-Koehler.

—— (2002). *Turning to one another: Simple conversations to restore hope to the future.* San Francisco: Berrett-Koehler.

Wheatley, Margaret J., and Myron Kellner-Rogers (1996). *A simpler way.* San Francisco: Berrett-Koehler.

Wilber, Ken (2000). *A theory of everything: An integral vision for business, politics, science, and spirituality.* Boston: Shambhala.

POETRY

Bly, Robert, James Hillman, and Michael Meade (eds.) (1993). *The rag and bone shop of the heart: A poetry anthology*. New York: Harper Perennial.

Collins, Billy (1998). *Picnic, Lightning*. Pittsburgh, PA: University of Pittsburgh Press.

—— (2002). *Nine horses*. New York: Random House.

—— (2002). *Sailing alone around the room*. New York: Random House.

Felleman, Hazel (ed.) (1936). *The best loved poems of the American people*. New York: Doubleday.

Graham, Jorie (2002). *Never: Poems*. New York: ECCO.

Keillor, Garrison (2002). *Good Poems*. New York: Viking.

Machado, Antonio (1982). *Antonio Machado: Selected poems*. Edited by Alan S. Trueblood. Cambridge, MA: Harvard University Press.

Neruda, Pablo (1975). *Extravaganza*. New York: Farrar, Straus and Giroux.

—— (1970). *Pablo Neruda: Selected poems*. Edited by Nathaniel Tarn. Boston: Houghton Mifflin / Seymour Lawrence.

O'Donohue, John (1997). *Anam cara: A book of Celtic wisdom*. New York: Cliff Street Books.

—— (1999). *Eternal echoes: Exploring our yearning to belong*. New York: Cliff Street Books.

Oliver, Mary (1983). *American primitive*. Boston: Bay Back Books / Little, Brown.

—— (1986). *Dream work*. New York: Atlantic Monthly Press.

—— (1992). *New and selected poems*. Boston: Beacon.

—— (2002). *What do we know*. Cambridge, MA: DaCapo.

—— (2003). *Owls and other fantasies*. Boston: Beacon.

—— (2004). *Why I wake early*. Boston: Beacon Press.

Pinsky, Robert, and Maggie Dietz, editors (2000). *American's favorite poems*. New York: Norton.

——, editors (2002). *Poems to read: A new favorite poem project anthology*. New York: Norton.

Rich, Adrienne (2002). *The fact of a doorframe: Selected poems, 1950–2001*. New York: Norton.

Rilke, Rainer Maria (2000). *The essential Rilke*. Edited by Galway Kinnell and Hannah Liebman. New York: Ecco.

—— (1989). *The selected poetry of Rainer Maria Rilke*. Edited by Stephen Mitchell. New York: Vintage.

Rumi (2002). *The soul of Rumi: A new collection of ecstatic poems*. Edited by Coleman Barks. New York: Harper San Francisco.

Szymborska, Wislawa (1995). *View with a grain of sand*. New York: Harcourt Brace.

—— (1998). *Poems new and collected*. New York: Harcourt.

—— (2001). *Miracle fair*. New York: Norton.

Thoreau, Henry David (1986). *Walden and civil disobedience*. New York: Penguin Classics.

Whyte, David (1999). *Fire in the earth*. Langley, WA: Many Rivers.

—— (2001). *Crossing the unknown sea*. New York: Riverhead Books.

—— (2002). *The heart aroused: Poetry and the preservation of the soul in corporate America* (2nd ed.) New York: Currency / Doubleday.

—— (2002). *House of belonging* (5th ed.). Langley, WA: Many Rivers.

Wood, Nancy (1993). *Spirit walker*. New York: Doubleday.

Permissions

Index

About the Author

George A. Goens is a senior partner with Goens/Esparo, LLC, which works with public- and private-sector organizations in leadership searches, leadership development, and accountability. He also serves as an associate with the Connecticut Association of Public School Superintendents. In addition, he has designed two charter schools for urban youth in Milwaukee.

Goens has served at all levels of public education. He taught social studies, served as an assistant principal and principal at the middle school level, gained central office administrative experience as a director of personnel, and served as the superintendent of two Wisconsin districts for over fourteen years. He also served as an associate professor in the doctoral program in educational leadership at the University of Hartford.

He has presented at the national American Association of School Administrators, Association for Supervisions and Curriculum Development, and National Staff Development Council conferences on leadership, change, and reform. He has written two other books; *Getting the Most from Public Schools* and *Mastering School Reform*, and has published more than fifty-five articles on supervision, change, and leadership.